A Basic Guide to

EQUESTRIAN

An Official U.S. Olympic Committee Sports Series

The U.S. Olympic Committee

Griffin Publishing

Griffin Publishing

544 Colorado Street
Glendale, California 91204

Telephone: 1-818-244-2128 / Fax 1-818-242-1172

Manufactured in the United States of America

Acknowledgments

PUBLISHER

Robert M. Howland
President, Griffin Publishing

U.S.O.C.

United States Olympic Committee
One Olympic Plaza
Colorado Springs, CO 80909-5760

SERIES EDITOR **Richard D. Burns, Ph.D.**
SENIOR EDITOR/WRITER **Joey Lorraine Parker**
PRODUCTION EDITOR **Larry Davis**
BOOK DESIGN **Mark M. Dodge**
PHOTO EDITOR **Robin L. Howland**
CONTRIBUTING EDITORS **American Grandprix Association**
Miller's Harness Co.
North American Riding for the
Handicapped Association, Inc.
United States Combined Training
Association, Inc.
United States Dressage Federation
United States Equestrian Team
United States Pony Clubs, Inc.

PHOTO CREDITS: Cover photo—James Leslie Parker; Rider—Michael Matz. Griffin Publishing wishes to thank the Contributing Editors and Hagerty Photography for photographic contributions.

Griffin Publishing wishes to thank the American Medical Association, the American Dental Association, Edward L. Garr, M.D. and Ray Padilla, D.D.S. for their contributions.

Editorial Statement

In the interest of brevity, the Editors have chosen to use the standard English form of address. Please be advised that this usage is not meant to suggest a restriction to, nor an endorsement of, any individual or group of individuals, either by age, gender, or athletic ability. The Editors certainly acknowledge that boys and girls, men and women, of every age and physical condition are actively involved in sports and we encourage everyone to enjoy the sports of his or her choice.

On behalf of the United States Olympic Committee,

Welcome to the Olympic Sports Series

We are extremely pleased to inaugurate the Olympic Sports Series. This unique series will encourage parents, athletes of all ages and novices who are thinking about a sport for the first time, to get involved with the challenging and rewarding world of Olympic sports.

This series of paperback books covers both summer and winter sports, features Olympic history and basic sports fundamentals, and encourages family involvement. Each book includes information on how to get started in a particular sport, including equipment and clothing; rules of the game; health and fitness; basic first aid; and guidelines for spectators. Of special interest is the information on opportunities for senior citizens, volunteers and physically challenged athletes. In addition, each book is enhanced by photographs and illustrations and a complete, easy-to-understand glossary.

Because this family-oriented series neither assumes nor requires prior knowledge of a particular sport it can be enjoyed by all age groups. Regardless of anyone's level of sports knowledge, playing experience or athletic ability, this official U.S. Olympic Committee Sports Series will encourage understanding and participation in sports and fitness.

The purchase of these books will assist the 1996 U.S. Olympic Team. This series supports the Olympic mission and serves importantly to enhance participation in the Olympic and Pan American Games.

John Krimsky, Jr.
Deputy Secretary General

Contents

U S A

An Athelete's Creed

The most important thing in the Olympic Games is not to win but to take part, just as the most important thing in life is not the triumph but the struggle. The essential thing is not to have conquered but to have fought well.

These famous words, commonly referred to as the Olympic Creed, were once spoken by Baron Pierre de Coubertin, founder of the modern Olympic Games. Whatever their origins, they aptly describe the theme behind each and every Olympic competition.

1

EQUESTRIAN GAMES IN THE OLYMPICS

For many sports, international competition was established with the modern Olympics in 1896. Equestrian games, however, did not appear in Olympic competition until 1912 when the Olympics took place in Stockholm, Sweden.

In 1906, Count Clarence von Rosen, a well-traveled and highly accomplished horseman and officially "Master of the Horse" to the King of Sweden, saw Olympic equestrian competition as a means of improving and promoting horsemanship worldwide. In a proposal sent to the International Olympic Committee (IOC) in 1907, von Rosen explained his theory and requested that equestrian events be included in upcoming Olympiads. In fact, he wanted the equestrian competition to begin as early as the 1908 Olympics scheduled for London, England.

The IOC agreed. Equestrian events were added to the program and announcements were sent. Unfortunately, no one correctly estimated the enthusiasm with which this news would be met. The

Committee thought perhaps 24 to 30 horses would register to compete and planned accordingly. When 88 horses from eight different nations appeared it took the IOC by storm! No one had anticipated such an eager response and there simply wasn't any place available to stable and exercise that many horses. An equally pressing problem was one of logistics in that each nation had its own idea as to how the events should be judged. With so much commotion, the IOC felt it had no other choice than to cancel the equestrian competition.

Although it seemed the horses had made the long trip for nothing, the high level of interest convinced Count von Rosen that competitors and spectators alike wanted international equestrian events. Far from giving up, he immediately went to work planning a successful equestrian competition for the upcoming 1912 Olympics.

In 1909 Count von Rosen formed an international committee to select which equestrian events would be included and to decide on a uniform standard of judging. One of the members of the committee was Prince Carl of Sweden, himself an avid horseman and host of the upcoming Games. Prince Carl acted as spokesman for the committee and encouraged other nations to support the establishment of equestrian events in Olympic competition. With the help of Prince Carl, Count von Rosen's committee was successful and equestrian events made their long-awaited Olympic debut in the 1912 Games in Stockholm.

International competition was still in its infancy, however, and the high cost of transporting horses around the world prohibited many of the European countries from sending teams to the 1932 Games in Los Angeles. Equestrian competitions were again disrupted during World War II, and for a few years it appeared as though Count von Rosen's efforts were destined to fail. After the War, however, the Olympic Games resumed in 1948 with renewed vigor, and equestrian events were once again part of the program. Throughout the world since the 1948 Games in London, equestrian events have grown in participation and popularity with each Olympiad.

Originally, entries for the equestrian games were exclusively from military cavalry units. Today, of course, military units have been replaced by civilian riders. Moreover, for many years only men rode in Olympic equestrian events, but in 1952, Marjorie B. Haynes became the first female member of the United States Equestrian Team and represented her country at the 1952 Games in Helsinki, Finland. That same year another woman rider, Lis Hartel of Denmark, won the individual silver medal in dressage. Today almost half of the riders competing in international competitions are women. Moreover, men and women ride together as teammates, and also compete against each other as equals.

Modern Olympic equestrian competition consists of three separate disciplines: Dressage, Three-Day Eventing, and Show Jumping. In each discipline medals are awarded for both team achievement and individual achievement. Although there have been minor changes in format over the years, these are the same three disciplines originally selected by Count von Rosen for the 1912 Olympics. Let's take a closer look at each of these Olympic equestrian events.

Dressage

The origin of this type of classical training for horses can be traced to the third and fourth century Greeks. The ancient Greeks studied the systematic training of their horses both as an artistic accomplishment and as a means of improving the performance of their cavalry. The Greeks correctly realized that an easily controlled horse, one responsive to his rider's every wish, would be the most valuable type of horse a soldier could ride. If a trooper was mounted on a horse he could not control he was of no help at all to his fellow soldiers. Therefore, with an eye toward improving the cavalry, Greek horsemen went to work devising a systematic approach to horse management.

Most notable among these early Greek horsemasters was General Xenophon who wrote two of the first known books on horse training. In this modern world of constant change it's interesting to note that much of Xenophon's theory on riding and training horses is as accurate and valuable now as it was in his own time. Today General Xenophon's style of classical riding and training is called dressage.

Dressage is actually a French word, and was not widely used to describe classical horse training until the early eighteenth century. It is derived from the French verb *dresser*, which means "to train or to adjust." The ultimate goal of dressage training is to produce a horse that works in perfect harmony with its rider.

Xenophon, the Greek cavalry officer who laid the foundations of classical dressage. His teachings are as applicable today as they were in his own era.

Dressage competitions test the harmonious development of the horse's physique and ability, and demand a high degree of understanding between horse and rider. In the Olympics, competitors must ride the Grand Prix test, the most advanced international test. Each rider is given the same amount of time to complete the test and all competitors must ride the same test. The test requires riders and their horses to demonstrate a prescribed variety of movements and figures. Entries are judged on how well they execute those required movements.

Photo: Jackson Shirley for USDF

USA's Carol Lavell riding Gifted at the 1990 World Equestrian Games in Stockholm, Sweden

Points To Look For

If you are interested in finding a horse suitable for dressage, these are some points you should look for. A well trained horse should be energetic and show a keen interest in its work, yet be under the rider's control and willing to carry out the rider's commands without resistance. The horse should move along with active, energetic steps, yet it should not "jig" or show other signs of disobedience. The hind legs should step well under the body and the back should be slightly rounded in a convex (never concave) fashion to accept the rider's weight. The neck should be long and arched with the head carried perpendicular to the ground. Almost any breed of horse can be trained in dressage, however, the larger European breeds, such as the German Hanoverian or Swedish Warmblood, are especially popular and well-suited for this discipline.

Three-Day Eventing

Many equine enthusiasts consider three-day eventing the complete test for horse and rider as it covers all aspects of horsemanship and training: obedience and calmness in the dressage phase; boldness and speed across country in the endurance phase; and stamina in the stadium jumping phase. A rider must ride the same horse in all phases of the three-day event.

Phase 1

The dressage test is held the first day. The objective of the dressage test is to demonstrate the harmonious development between horse and rider. This is a difficult phase of the three-day event, in part because event horses are exceptionally keen, athletic individuals, anxious to get going on the cross country course. It is the rider's objective to demonstrate that although his horse is fit and ready to gallop and jump cross country, the horse is still obedient and willing to perform the intricate maneuvers of the dressage test without showing resistance or impatience. Moreover, a good dressage test score puts a rider among the leaders and gives him a decided advantage going into the second phase of the competition.

Photo: V. J. Zabek for USCTA

Young riders like Heather Koehler prepare for combined training competition

Phase 2

The endurance phase is held on the second day. The objective is to prove the speed, endurance and cross country jumping ability of the horse and to test the rider's knowledge of timing and pace control. Penalties are incurred for falls or refusals at the obstacles, for going off the course, and for exceeding the time allowed.

The endurance competition has four parts: A) roads and tracks; B) steeplechase; C) roads and tracks again; and D) cross country. Each part is assigned a "time allowed," that means the rider's goal is to complete that part of the competition within the time, yet must do so without over exerting the horse. Timing is very important in the endurance phase. The rider does not want to ask more of his horse than absolutely necessary in each part so that the horse will have enough energy left to complete the entire competition.

Veterinarians check the horses at regular intervals and if a veterinarian feels a horse is getting too tired, he can order the rider to give the horse a rest period of a designated length of time. If the horse still is not ready to continue or if the veterinarian feels a horse is unfit, he can withdraw that animal from the competition. As you can see, it's very important for a rider to practice timing and pace control to be able to make the best use of his horse's energy and ability.

Phase 3

The stadium jumping phase is held on the third and final day. Unlike the endurance, this phase of the competition is held inside an arena, hence the term "stadium jumping." The objective is to test the horse's ability to bounce back after the endurance competition. Many times riders are tied in number of points at the end of the dressage and endurance phases, so the stadium jumping phase ultimately decides the winner.

Points To Look For

If you are interested in finding a horse suitable for three-day eventing, these are some points you should look for. A three-day event horse must be sound, healthy and strong. Almost any breed of horse can be used, but long-striding horses, such as Thoroughbreds, are among those most favored. This is because their long legs, sloping pasterns and well-angled shoulders enable them to cover the ground most efficiently. A horse for this discipline must be obedient, not only to score well on the dressage test, but even more importantly, to be safe to ride and jump in the endurance and stadium jumping phases of the competition. Finally, the horse must move freely forward and jump willingly—a horse that has to be coaxed over every obstacle is not going to make it as a three-day event competitor.

Show Jumping

Show jumping is one of the most crowd-pleasing of all equestrian disciplines. Far from the subjective, analytical judging used in dressage, show jumping is judged objectively—that is, the horse either clears the obstacle and completes the course within the time allowed, or he doesn't. Of course, there are a few more technicalities, but basically that's how show jumping is scored. Because of that objective approach, even first-time horse show attendees can quickly understand what's happening on the field.

In show jumping, the horse's athletic ability and the rider's skill are tested over a course of obstacles. A competitor accumulates penalty points, called *faults*, for errors such as knocking down an obstacle, getting a hoof in the water, and/or failing to jump an obstacle. Moreover, the course must be completed within a designated time allowed. The object is to complete the course as quickly as possible without accruing any faults.

Before the start of a show jumping competition, each rider is permitted to walk the course on foot and inspect each fence. What a rider learns about a course during this inspection walk becomes an important part of his strategy. The rider will determine the best location for a turn or the best possible approach to clear a particular obstacle.

Photo: AGA

USA's Katie Monahan Prudent, three-time "AGA Rider of the Year," 1982, 1986, and 1988

Once the inspection walk has been completed, no one is allowed on the course again until the competition begins. Once the show begins, only mounted competitors, performing in their appointed order, are allowed in the arena.

Each entry is assigned a number. The numbers are put into a hat and the starting order is determined by a draw. When a rider's number is called, he or she enters the arena already mounted. The rider is not allowed to cross the starting line until the judge gives the starting signal.

In some competitions, the first round is not judged against the clock but is used as an elimination round. Only competitors with a no-fault first round are allowed to continue. Subsequent rounds *are* judged against the clock, where time as well as faults determine the winner.

Points To Look For

If you're interested in buying a show jumper, look for a horse with tremendous athletic ability, especially in regards to lengthening and shortening its stride. Jumpers have to be able to make micro-second adjustments in their approach to an obstacle, so a horse with a smooth, "elastic" stride is essential. Also, a jumper must be responsive to the rider's every command. A horse that ignores his rider and simply plows ahead won't be able to make the tight turns found on today's highly technical jumper courses.

Almost any breed horse can jump a few small fences, but for advanced show jumping competitions such as the Olympics and the World Cup, Thoroughbreds and warmbloods are most often used. Their natural athletic ability is well-suited for grand prix jumping.

Gate

Hog's back

Rustic

Brush

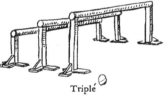

Triple

Painted panel and poles

Chicken coop

Post and rail

Course obstacles

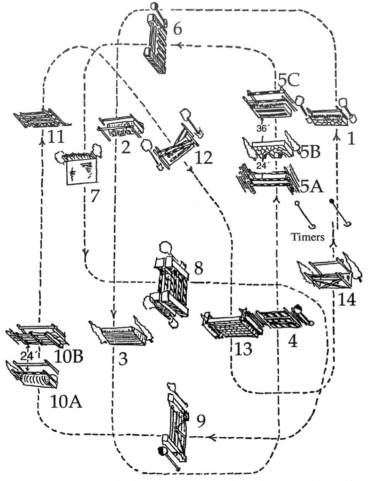

24´ means two strides between 5A and 5B, and 10A and 10B
36´ means three strides between 5B and 5C

Today's grand prix courses are highly technical

Jumps on Grand Prix Course

1. Brush and rails
2. Chicken coop and rails
3. Vertical wall
4. Vertical planks
5. First combination on the course—
   5a. Three-rail spread
   5b. Stone wall
   5c. Brush and rails
6. Gate and rails
7. Water jump
8. Rails over planks
9. Vertical gate
10. Second combination on the course—
    10a. Rails over a barrel
    10b. Planks with hidden rail behind
11. Vertical planks
12. Swedish oxer
13. Vertical wall
14. Rails over a liverpool

2

Selecting a Riding School

No matter what your level of experience with horses, a good riding school can be your best friend. You can take lessons from qualified instructors; you'll have access to facilities such as well-footed riding rings, bath racks, and hot walkers; your horse will have access to top professionals in veterinary medicine, horseshoeing, transportation (if you go to horse shows), and training; and, perhaps most important, there will be experienced horsemen around to assist you in an emergency. You'll make friends with people who like horses just as much as you do and you'll always have someone to ride with. Note—it is especially important to have a riding buddy if you are heading out on unfamiliar trails. A good riding school can give you all of these benefits, and more.

Finding A Stable

If you are new to riding or have recently moved to a new location, you'll want to know how to find stables in your area. You can try the phone book, but most training barns don't advertise in general directories. Use the phone book to locate tack and feed stores in your area. Call or visit your neighborhood tack and feed dealer. Tack shop owners always know where the best training barns are located and can be a gold mine of information. Write down the names and phone numbers they give you, then call the barns and make an appointment to visit. Tell the barn you would like to meet the staff during your visit and would they please arrange it so you can have a short conference with the instructor, trainer and/or stable manager. Note—if you just show up at the barn without calling, the instructor may be teaching a class or schooling a horse. It's not fair to expect him or her to stop everything if they didn't know you were coming. Call first and confirm the best time for you to visit.

If you can't find a tack or feed store in the phone book, try the office of an equine veterinarian. For professional reasons a vet's office may be reluctant to divulge information about any particular establishment, but if you explain that you are new to horses or new to the area and you're completely lost, they may give you the names of some barns to contact. Note—a lot of your success depends on how politely you present yourself. Realize, too, that should the vet's office be in the middle of an emergency, they simply won't have time to talk to you. Don't be offended, simply thank them, hang up, and try again in a day or two.

If none of those approaches work for you, try locating a training stable outside your immediate area. Explain your situation and see if they can recommend anyone closer to you. If you subscribe to any equine magazines, check the classified listings, or call the magazine and ask if they know of any stables in your area. If you live near a college or university, contact their athletic department and ask if they have a riding program. If so, someone in the riding group should be able to help you.

Once you have located the stables in your area, it's up to you to arrange to visit each one, then select the one that best meets your needs.

Let's take a closer look at points to consider.

Benefits, Safety, and Costs

Both horse and rider benefit from being with a quality riding stable. If you own your own horse and board at the riding stable, the horse will be supervised during the hours that you cannot be with him. Should your horse become ill or injured, someone will be there to tend to his immediate care and call the veterinarian, if necessary. You will know that your horse will always have fresh water and will be fed properly and on time. These facts alone give any responsible horse owner added peace of mind, but both horse and rider benefit in other ways as well. In a top stable you will have access to a variety of aids such as safe, well-constructed jumps, good riding arenas, hot walkers, bath racks, cross ties, bull pens, lettered dressage courts, tack rooms, pasture or turn-out pens, and clean feed rooms. In addition, you can take lessons from qualified instructors and your horse will be serviced by competent professionals for all veterinary and shoeing needs. All of these things are benefits, both to you and to your horse.

The safety factor is fairly obvious in that should an emergency arise, you won't be left alone to deal with a frightening or stressful situation. Moreover, top barns demand that horses be handled properly and that basic safety rules be followed at all times. You can learn a great deal about how to handle a horse by being with a good barn where high standards are maintained. If you are new to riding, these standards may seem nit-picky at first. They are not—they are there to ensure the safety and well being of all horses, riders, and visitors. You will soon learn the rationale for *why* things must be done (or not done) a certain way. Later on, if you choose to keep your horse at home, you will know how to handle him in a safe and effective manner.

Different stables offer different services, and the cost of riding with a particular establishment often corresponds to the services available. If you are interested in trail riding, look for a barn with access to good trails, and ask if you'll have the chance to ride out with more experienced horsemen. If the answer to the first two questions is yes, you know you're at least on the right track. If you are interested in riding in horse shows, look for a barn that either puts on its own horse shows or travels to shows on a fairly regular basis. That way you'll be with a barn that can give you the showing experience you need.

Once you have found a stable that offers the type of riding you enjoy, the next step is to look around the stable and evaluate it for general safety and cleanliness. Will your horse have the type of accommodations you want him to have? Will he be fed at approximately the same time each day? Regular feeding is important to your horse's health, so be sure to ask about the feeding schedule. Will your horse have constant access to fresh water? Will there be a secure place for you to keep your tack and equipment? If you regularly visit the barn after dark, you'll want to ask about lighting. Are the rings lighted for night riding? What about lights in the barns, grooming area, and parking lot? All of these are points to consider.

No stable in the world can accommodate every rider's wishes. The secret to finding the right stable for you is to know where you are willing to be flexible and where you should not compromise. For example, if you know that you'll be riding in the evenings after dark, security and lighting are vital, these are not points on which you can compromise. If trail riding is your primary reason for having a horse, you probably wouldn't be happy in an urban stable with no access to the out-of-doors. By knowing your own goals and objectives before you go stable shopping, you'll be able to make better decisions about which facility is right for you.

Horses and Instructors

If you do not yet own a horse, you'll need to find a riding school that has lesson horses for you to ride. Don't underestimate the importance of a good lesson horse, you'll be amazed at all it has to teach you. No top rider in the world ever started out on an Olympic-level horse, they first had to learn the basics from an experienced school horse. Moreover, most top competitors credit their success to what they learned from their lesson horses almost as much as from their instructors.

When you visit a stable, ask to see the lesson horses. Are they healthy, clean, and well-maintained? Look carefully at the hooves, are they neatly trimmed? Do the shoes appear to fit? Chances are, the answers to these questions will be yes. Top stables know the value of their school horses and they take good care of their stock. If you're lucky enough to arrive while a lesson is in progress, sit quietly and watch for a few minutes. Do the riders appear to be having a good time as well as learning? If the answer to this question is also yes, you're in the right place.

Photo: Dawn Johnson for USPC

A young rider gets valuable tips from her instructor

Riding instructors have special areas of interest just as do academic instructors, so you may find it helpful to ride with an instructor who shares your goals and objectives. Realize, however, that regardless of any special interest, good riding is always based in sound fundamentals. If possible, watch the instructor teach a few lessons. Do the riders wear safety hats and boots or other appropriate footwear? Are the instructor's directions clear and easy to understand? (You may not understand some of the terminology if you're watching an advanced class, but if the *students* understand, they have learned the terms along the way. So will you.) Finally, what are the costs per lesson and how many times per week are you expected to ride? If these factors fit into your schedule and budget, sign up for lessons as soon as you can. You'll be glad you did.

Centers for Handicapped Riders

Horseback riding and other equine activities provide challenges as well as rewards for all riders, but for a handicapped rider, the challenges are even greater. The North American Riding for the Handicapped Association (NARHA) was formed specifically to help disabled men, women, and children successfully meet these challenges. Founded in 1969 and headquartered in Denver, Colorado, NARHA is dedicated to serving individuals of all ages afflicted with mental, physical, and emotional disabilities. NARHA has more than 450 operating centers throughout the Untied States and Canada, ranging from small, one-person programs to large operations with a full staff of instructors and therapists.

Therapeutic riding is recognized by the American Occupational Therapy Association and the American Physical Therapy Association. The benefits of therapeutic riding are available to individuals with almost any disability, and research shows that students who participate in therapeutic riding experience physical, emotional and mental rewards.

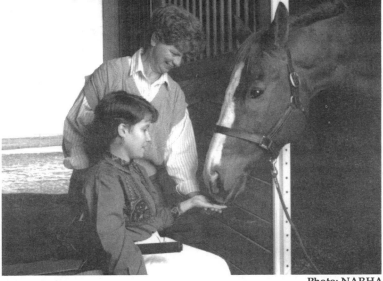

Photo: NARHA

**NARHA means opportunities for handicapped
horse enthusiasts.**

For individuals with impaired mobility, horseback
riding gently and rhythmically moves their bodies in
a manner similar to walking, thereby improving their
balance, muscle control and overall strength.

In addition to therapeutic riding, many NARHA
operating centers offer additional equine activities for
the handicapped including carriage driving, vaulting,
hippotherapy, trail riding, equestrian competitions,
and/or a study in stable management.

Individuals with learning or mental disabilities are
motivated by riding to increase concentration,
patience and discipline. If a psychological or
emotional disability is present, the unique
relationship formed with a horse can help improve

interpersonal relationships, and everyone benefits from increased self-esteem and coping skills. NARHA sets and maintains high safety standards, provides continuing education, and offers networking opportunities for individual and operating center members. Horses and ponies participating in NARHA programs are safe, well schooled, and suitable to the task at hand. Handicapped riders do not need to supply their own horse; NARHA provides each rider with a horse compatible with his/her size and ability.

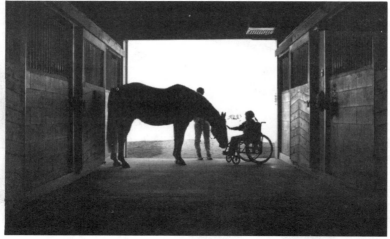

Photo: NARHA

Emotional well-being comes from time spent with horses

Operating centers need volunteers, riders, instructors, therapists, horses and equipment. For information on enrolling an individual in the therapeutic riding program, donating a horse or equipment, or becoming a financial donor or riding center volunteer, contact the NARHA.

Youth Groups

One of the best ways for young enthusiasts to learn about riding and horse care is to join a youth group involved with equestrian activities. One such group is the United States Pony Club (USPC). The USPC uses the term "pony" to reflect its youthful membership, not the size of the animal. Horses and ponies of many different breeds and sizes are seen in Pony Club activities and, in some clubs, a member does not have to own a horse or pony to belong.

Photo: Susan Showalter for USPC

**Pony Club reflects its youthful membership,
not the size of the animal.**

Prior knowledge of horses is not required for Pony Club membership. One or more qualified instructors are a part of every Pony Club and members learn riding skills, stable management, basic veterinary care and, eventually, competition riding. There are also non-riding activities in which clubs compete in quizbowl competitions which test members' knowledge about horses and horse care. The emphasis is on fun as well as on education.

The United States Pony Club is the leading junior equestrian organization in the world, and is represented in 30 countries. In the U.S. there are more than 570 individual clubs throughout the country with more than 11,000 members. Membership is open to any individual up to the age of twenty-one, and volunteers of any age are always welcome. The primary objective of the Pony Club is to provide instruction in riding and horsemanship, with an emphasis on safety procedures, and to instill in members the ideal of good sportsmanship and the knowledge which will enable them to properly care for and enjoy horses all their lives. For more information contact the USPC.

USET Young Riders Program

Since 1965, the Rolex/USET Show Jumping Talent Search program has sought to educate as well as test its young participants, encouraging them to develop lasting skills while producing world-class show jumping riders for future USET squads.

Open to riders up to 21-years-old who have qualified through their placement in regional Rolex/USET Show Jumping Talent Search classes, the program's Finals ask riders to demonstrate that they can successfully execute four varied and difficult phases of show jumping. Phase I tests their knowledge of "flat" work, *i.e.*, without fences; Phase II tests their ability over an intensive gymnastics course; Phase III has riders jumping grand prix-style fences, which may include natural obstacles such as a ditch, liverpool, or water jump; Phase IV, modeled after the Show Jumping World Championship, consists of a ride-off among the top four finishers, with competitors riding first their own horse, then each other's horses, over the same course.

Special USET Medals are awarded in recognition of wins. The Rolex/USET Show Jumping Talent Search program represents an innovative approach to training young riders and has done much to raise the standards of horsemanship over the past three decades. The program bodes well for continuing a legacy of international success for the USET which already includes an impressive 21 Olympic and 48 Pan American Games Medals in equestrian competition. For mor information, contact the USET.

Scholastic Riding Programs

Throughout the nation, high schools, colleges, and universities are forming riding programs and interscholastic equestrian teams. Perhaps one of the best known programs is the Intercollegiate Horse Show Association and its National Championships, sponsored by Miller's.

Established in 1967 by Robert E. Cacchione, then a student at Fairleigh Dickenson University, the IHSA is founded on the principal that any college student should be able to participate in horse shows regardless of his or her financial status or riding experience. The IHSA promotes competition for riders of all skill levels who compete individually and as teams at Regional and National events.

Photo: Miller's

**Intercollegiate Horse Show Association trophy
sponsored by Miller's**

The competition is unique in that all riders are mounted on horses supplied by the host college, each horse being drawn by lot. Some top names in the sport who have shown for their college teams include Greg Best, University of Pennsylvania; Beezie Patton, Southern Virginia College for Women; and Peter Wylde, Tufts University.

For more information on scholastic riding programs, contact the athletic department of the high school, college, or university of your choice. If they don't already have a riding program, perhaps you could be the person to start one!

List of Equestrian Associations

American Grandprix Association (AGA)
3104 Cherry Palm Drive, Suite 220
Tampa, FL 33619   Phone: (800) 237-8924

American Horse Shows Association (AHSA)
220 East 42nd Street, Suite 409
New York, NY 10017-5876   Phone: (212) 972-2472

Intercollegiate Horse Show Association (IHSA)
c/o Miller's
117 E. 24th Street
New York, NY 10010   Phone: (212) 673-1400

**North American Riding for the
Handicapped Association (NARHA)**
P. O. Box 33150
Denver, CO 80233   Phone: (303) 452-1212

United States Combined Training Association (USCTA)
461 Boston Road, Suite D-6
Topsfield, MA 01983-1295   Phone: (508) 887-9090

United States Dressage Federation (USDF)
7700 A Street
Lincoln, NE 68510   Phone: (402) 434-8550

United States Equestrian Team (USET)
Pottersville Road
Gladstone, NJ 07934   Phone: (908) 234-1251

United States Pony Club (USPC)
Kentucky Horse Park
4071 Iron Works Pike
Lexington, KY 40511   Phone: (606) 254-7669

USET Olympic Medal Highlights

Since the 1912 Games, the United States has won 37 Olympic Medals in Equestrian. Of that total, 26 have been won since 1952, the year the USET assumed responsibility for selecting, training and fielding American Equestrian Teams.

1952 Helsinki, Finland
    (2) Bronze Jumping Team, Three-Day Team

1960 Rome, Italy
    (1) Silver   Jumping Team

1964 Tokyo, Japan
    (1) Silver   Three-Day Team

1968 Mexico City, Mexico
    (1) Gold   William Steinkraus/Snowbound, Individual Jumping
    (1) Silver   Three-Day Team
    (1) Bronze Michael Page/Foster, Three-Day Individual

1972 Munich, West Germany
    (2) Silver   Jumping Team, Three-Day Team
    (1) Bronze Neal Shapiro/Sloopy, Individual Jumping

1976 Montreal, Canada
    (2) Gold   Tad Coffin/Bally Cor, Individual Three-Day,
               Three-Day Team
    (1) Silver   J. Michael Plumb/Better and Better, Ind. Three-Day
    (1) Bronze Dressage Team

1980 Alternate Games, Rotterdam, Holland
    (1)Bronze Melanie Smith/Calypso, Individual Jumping

1980 Alternate Games, Fontainebleau, France
    (1) Silver   James Wofford/Catawich, Individual Three-Day
    (1) Bronze Torrance Watkins/Poltroon, Individual Three-Day

1984 Los Angeles, United States
    (2) Gold   Joe Fargis/Touch of Class, Individual Jumping,
                Three-Day Team, Jumping Team,
    (2) Silver   Conrad Homfeld/Abdullah, Individual Jumping,
                Karen Stives/Ben Arthur, Individual Three-Day

1988 Seoul, South Korea
    (2) Silver   Greg Best/Gem Twist, Individual Jumping,
                Jumping Team,

1992 Barcelona, Spain
    (2) Bronze Norman Dello Joio/Irish, Individual Jumping,
                Dressage Team

 3

A HORSE OF YOUR OWN

Are you already anticipating the day you will get your first horse? If so, you are not alone. Horseback riding is one of the most popular and fastest growing sports in America. In fact, it may surprise you to learn that more commercial stables are opening up in urban areas than in rural areas, and that's especially good news for city-dwelling horse lovers. After all, one of the big advantages of a commercial stable is that you can get the supervised help you'll need to get started right.

Of course, if you live in a rural area and plan to keep your horse at home, you already have something city dwellers can only imagine: access to open space. Perhaps your dream is to canter your new horse across a green meadow, explore a path through the woods, walk beside a mountain stream, or take a brisk, early-morning trot when desert wildflowers are in full bloom. No matter where you live, trail riding allows you to develop a special communication with your horse that no amount of ring work can ever surpass. If you are fortunate enough to be able to take lessons from a qualified instructor *and* have access to a few trails, you really will have the best of both worlds.

If you haven't already purchased an animal, the following may be helpful to you in making your selection.

Goals and Objectives

Probably the single most important issue is to decide what it is you want to accomplish with your new horse. What are your goals and objectives? This may seem obvious, but the issue is complex and deserves a thorough examination. There are many forms of riding and many things that can be accomplished, but to be successful in your endeavor you must first have a horse that is suitable to your purpose. This does *not* mean the most expensive nor the biggest nor even the "prettiest" horse—it does, however, mean finding the horse best suited to meeting your needs. Remember that horses, like people, are different from one another, not only in size, shape and hair color, but in temperament, too. The secret to success is to find a horse that has the experience, athletic ability and personality to meet your goals and objectives.

Trail Riding

If your goal is to meander along the trail, savoring the beauties of nature (and that can be a rewarding goal in and of itself), then you need a horse that enjoys being away from the barn, doesn't shy or spook easily, will stand quietly while you mount and dismount, is willing to cross streams, climb rocks, or go up and down hills and, most importantly, is not afraid of traffic. If this is your first horse, it's best to purchase one that has experience with all of these situations and has proven himself to be a quiet, competent trail horse.

A perfect match — this horse and rider are obviously well-suited to each other

It's not fun to ride a horse so nervous he jigs every step of the way, nor so "barn sour" that he won't take a step without constant and vigorous encouragement from his rider. You want a horse you can have fun with. Leave the difficult horses to the more experienced riders—after all, your goal is to have safe, enjoyable trail rides, not pitched battles! A seasoned, well-behaved horse will prove to be a trust-worthy companion and a wonderful teacher.

Pleasure Horses

Although some breeds seem to be especially popular for trail riding almost any breed can be used for this purpose. The individual animal is what's important here, not the breed. Look for experience, athletic ability and temperament, and don't let yourself get sidetracked with fancy breeding records.

Photo: Gary R. Coppage for USPC

Horse and rider enjoy a day away from the barn

When selecting a trail horse it is advisable to consider the horse's size relative to your size. If you select an animal so tall you can't mount without assistance, you're going to be up a creek without a paddle if you ever have to dismount to open and close a gate or move an object blocking the trail. You don't want to have to walk all the way home because you couldn't get back on!

One of the most popular breeds for both trail riding and horse shows is the American Quarter Horse. His conformation, way of moving, and quiet temperament makes the Quarter Horse an excellent choice for riders of all ages and levels of experience.

Performance Horses

If you goal is to compete in horse shows, combined training events, gymkhanas or other equestrian competitions, you will need to be more concerned about the breed of horse you select. Specific types of performance require specific types of athletic ability, and certain breeds are naturally better at some things than they are at others.

Depending on your goals and objectives, you may even have to consider switching from one breed or type of horse to another. For example, if you've been riding a long-legged Thoroughbred, but decide you want to show in western pleasure classes, you're going to have to select another horse—one suitable to the slow, short-striding type of movement desired in the western performance horse. Conversely, if you've been riding a small, short-striding horse, but now you want to ride jumpers, you'll need a horse with the athletic ability to leap the obstacles *and* easily cover the distance between fences. A short-legged horse will have a harder time turning in a clean performance and a fast time on a jumper course than will a taller, longer-striding animal.

Some breed associations have their own horse shows. At a breed-specific show, you would need to ride a horse of that particular breed. At non-breed specific shows, you may ride a horse of any breed, but you would still want to select a horse well-suited to that particular activity.

Photo: V. J. Zabek for USCTA

An athletic horse well-suited to the requirements of combined training.

If you're not sure yet what type of riding most appeals to you, spend some time going to a variety of equestrian events. Take in a dressage show and watch the riders and horses "dance as one" in the beautiful musical kur. Visit an Arabian show and watch the native costume class where riders dressed in elaborate Arabian regalia enter the arena at a full gallop—a truly spectacular sight. Go to a western show and observe the quiet, rhythmic action of the pleasure and trail horses, and compare that to the hair-raising spins and slides of the stock horses. For pure heart-stopping action, however, nothing beats grand prix jumping. Attending a grand prix gives you a good opportunity to see and compare warmbloods and Thoroughbreds, and to notice how the different breeds are ridden. Generally, the warmbloods take a little more leg and "push," while the Thoroughbreds are usually ridden with great finesse and a light seat.

Photo: Jackson Shirley for USDF

European warmbloods like this Hanoverian gelding make elegant dressage horses. Photo: Three-time OlympianRobert Dover on Walzertakt at 1990 World Equestrian Games

Since every experience around horses will help you increase your knowledge, try to attend as many different horse shows as you can. Some breed-specific shows, such as Arabian and Morgan, have classes for all three major divisions: hunt seat, stock seat (or western), and saddle seat. Remember, for breed-specific shows and activities, you will need a horse of that particular breed. At open, or non-breed-specific shows, you will see a variety of breeds being ridden, but all will be horses well-suited to that particular type of work.

Whenever you are watching equestrian events, pay close attention to the horses themselves and ask yourself two questions: Do these look like horses I would want to ride? Is this style of riding something I would want to do? Answering these questions can help you focus and define your riding goals and objectives.

It will take lots of practice to ride well enough to actually enter a competition, but visiting horse shows now is an excellent way to learn about different breeds and different styles of riding. Last but not least, watching the great horses and riders gives you incentive to work hard in your riding lessons. Remember, no one ever woke up one morning suddenly "knowing" how to ride. The champions got to *be* champions because they worked at it!

STABLE
MANAGEMENT

Half the fun of owning a horse is taking care of him. Before you buy or lease a horse, decide where your horse will live and how often you can get there to take care of him. If possible, try to stable your horse close to home so that you can check on him every day. Your horse depends on you to provide him with a clean, safe environment; to give him the food, water, and nutritional supplements that his body needs; to provide prompt veterinary aid in the event of an emergency; and to keep his hooves clean, trimmed, and shod on a regular basis. If your circumstances are such that you can only visit your horse on weekends, you will have to arrange for someone to watch him during the week—domesticated horses simply cannot be left to their own devices. The reason is that if your horse should become ill or injured, or even tangled in the fence, you wouldn't know it until the weekend, and your horse can't wait that long for help. So, let's say that you have found three or four stables within your area from which to choose. Let's take a closer look at the things you'll want to consider.

Facilities

The four most important considerations are: 1) the type of stabling your horse will have; 2) your access to riding arenas and trails; 3) the presence of on-site trainers, grooms and other able assistants; and 4) the availability of extras such as a hot walker, cross ties, tack and feed storage compartments, bath racks, turn-out areas, and lights.

Stabling

Basically, there are three types of stabling: 1) indoor stalls; 2) covered paddocks; and 3) open pasture. Of course there are variations on these basics, but in the main those are the most common types of stabling available.

Indoor Stalls—This refers to a box stall in a barn. The horse remains enclosed and under cover until someone takes him out—he cannot get out of the box stall by himself. Box stalls range in size from 8' x 10' to 14' x 16', with 12' x 12' being one of the most common. What's important here is that you get a stall large enough for your particular animal. A Connemara pony, for example, will fit nicely into an 8' x 10' stall, but you certainly couldn't stuff a Thoroughbred or a Hanoverian into one that size! If the barn has stalls of more than one size, make sure you tell the stable manager what breed of horse or pony you have and make sure you will be assigned a stall that meets your needs.

The points you should consider are how often and at what time of day can you visit your horse. If you can get down every day during the daylight hours, an interior stall will make no difference to your horse, but if you can only visit two or three times a week, and even then only in the evening, your horse will never see the sun. Such an arrangement is not healthy for a horse and you would need to be in a stable where your horse can be turned out-of-doors during the day.

Construction of the stall is also important. Both the door and the stall itself must be free from nails, sharp edges or other snags; and the door, regardless of style, should open and close smoothly and securely. If the stall contains a hay rick or feed bin, check it for rough edges. If you find any, ask that they be sanded or filed. Most barns today have automatic watering devices. Make sure the water float is working properly and that the bowl is free from leaks.

Covered Paddocks—Covered paddocks are not only popular at boarding and training stables, they make a secure shelter for horses kept at home; and a covered paddock is an economical alternative to building a full-scale barn. If you are considering building a covered paddock or boarding your horse at a stable where paddocks are available, the following guidelines may be helpful.

If you are looking at space at a boarding stable, be sure the paddock has a good roof covering at least one-third of the total area. A paddock without a roof is not suitable for permanent stabling. Your horse needs a place to get out of the sun and away from flies and other insects. Horses are capable of withstanding cold weather with no ill effect, but the hot summer sun dries the skin and fades the coat, and zaps a horse's energy. If possible, visit the stable both morning and afternoon. Check the angle of the sun and be sure that the roof's shadow falls *into* the paddock where your horse can take advantage of it— a shadow cast outside the paddock is of no benefit. Equally important are a clean and continuous supply of drinking water, good footing, adequate drainage, and a securely-latching gate.

Open Pasture—Regardless of size, the field must be safe for horses and ponies. The surrounding fence should be at least four feet high, strong enough to prevent escape, and made from a material that will not injure any animal that runs into it or leans against it. Barbed wire must never be used around horses. If the fence is sagging, weak, or in any way needs repair, renovations must be completed before animals can be turned out.

Check your pasture at least once a week for debris, and remove any foreign matter whenever you see it. Take a little wagon or a burlap sack around with you and load up—no matter how carefully you clean your pasture, horses hooves turn up rocks and other objects that may have been buried for years. For safety reasons, any deep holes should be filled before using the pasture, and low spots should be filled and graded as necessary. Low spots gather water, and standing water is a haven for mosquitoes and other harmful pests.

Salt licks should be available to pastured horses, and there should be more than one source of clean, readily-available drinking water. That way, if one source fails, another will be operable while the first is being repaired. Horses and ponies must NEVER be left without drinking water. They can and will become dehydrated very quickly if deprived of water.

Footing and Bedding

Footing refers to the ground in your riding arenas and exercise areas. As with your pasture, any holes or low places should be filled and graded. All rocks and other debris must be removed and the entire surface should be "combed" on a regular basis.

Whatever form of bedding you use in your stalls and covered paddocks, it should provide insulation, draw moisture, cushion the horse's feet (thereby reducing stress on his legs), and give him a soft bed on which he can lie down and rest. When the horse is lying down, his nose is close to the bedding; therefore, bedding cannot be of any substance which is overly dusty or which would disturb his breathing. Finally, bedding must be easy to clean. A foul, unkept stable is disgusting, especially so to the horses! Choose a bedding material that you can toss, clean, and carry away.

Straw is a good insulator and is especially popular as a bedding source in very cold climates. Straw has one drawback, however, in that horses tend to eat it. Since straw is not easy to digest, this may not be a good choice for some horses.

One of the most popular bedding materials is wood shavings. They are warm, clean, gentle on the legs, and economical to buy, either in bales or in bulk. If you buy in bulk, be sure to have an enclosed area for storage, otherwise the first big wind will blow them away. If you choose this source of bedding, make sure to use shavings, not sawdust. Sawdust is so fine that it can cause respiratory problems, and horses don't stay clean when sleeping on it.

Feed and Water

Hay is the staple of a horse's diet. Basically, there are two types of hay: grasses and legumes. Grass hays produce their seeds in "seed heads," legumes produce theirs in "flowers." Some well-known grass hays are timothy, red clover, Kentucky blue grass, and orchard grass. Perhaps the best-known legume hay is alfalfa. Different types of hay are available in different parts of the country. Grass hays are readily available in the Midwest, but alfalfa is more prevalent in the Southwest.

Buying Hay

When buying hay, look for clarity in color. Hay should be green and look healthy, without a trace of gray film on the stems or leaves. A gray color indicates mold, and horses must never be allowed to eat any hay (or grain) containing mold. Feel the stems and leaves; they should not feel damp or soggy, nor should they feel overly dry. Good hay bends without breaking, gently returning to its upright shape. If the stems snap like dry twigs, they probably are.

The most important test hay must pass is the "smell test"—good hay smells sweet, moldy hay emits a acrid, unpleasant order. Pull a flake apart and smell it, paying particular attention to the center. If it smells bad, don't buy it—not at any price. A nasty odor is a tell-tale sign of mold.

Feeding grass clippings is *not* the same as letting a horse graze on pasture grass. Grass molds and ferments very soon after cutting, and clippings have been known to cause serious illness. No matter how tasty they might look, grass clippings should never be fed to a horse or pony.

Storage

To keep it fresh, hay must be stored up off the ground or floor. Wooden pallets work very well, or you can lay two-by-sixes on the ground and stack the hay on top of them. Do not pack the bales tight against each other. Arrange them in a cross pattern to encourage air circulation, and always keep hay protected from rain, fog, or dampness. If hay is stored out-of-doors, a tarp over the hay rick provides good protection. If hay is kept indoors, the building or shed should have good ventilation, and keep bales from touching the walls where they can soak up moisture.

Feeding Schedule

Horses do best when given constant access to hay or pasture grass and are allowed to pick and nibble at liberty. This is how horses eat in the wild—wandering along, grazing throughout the day. Unfortunately, it is not always possible to feed domesticated horses this way. Keep your feeding schedule as constant as you possibly can. Your horse should always have at least one hour to digest his food before exercise, two hours is even better. Check his drinking water supply and clean and fill any buckets.

If you supplement your horse's diet with grain, make sure he is completely cool, relaxed and has had a chance to drink water before feeding grain. For the average horse as described above, 6 pounds of rolled oats, 3 pounds of rolled corn, along with a general vitamin/mineral supplement makes a nice post-workout meal. You can get fancy and top it off with sliced carrots and apples and your horse will think you're a regular Julia Child. But no matter how much your horse seems to enjoy it, grain is a supplement to, not a replacement for, hay, pasture grass, or other fiber. Feed good quality hay at regular, established feeding times, and you will have a healthy and happy partner.

Grain—For novice horse owners, a ready-mixed feed is probably the safest way to add grain to your horse's diet. There are many excellent brands on the market nationwide. Tell the feed store clerk what breed of horse you have, its age, what type of work it's doing, and how often. For example, the nutritional needs of a grand prix jumper will be different than those of a pleasure horse. Also mention if your horse is kept in a box stall or paddock, or if he is kept at pasture where he has plenty of room to roam. These questions are important because how your horse lives effects the quantity and type of food he should get. Follow the feeding directions on the label and feed at the same time every day.

Grain should be kept in a sealable container, away from excessive heat, dampness, and direct sunlight. If grain starts to mold it will emit a sour odor. Get rid of it! All of it. You must not feed from a bin where grain has started to mold. Grain bins should be stored on wooden blocks to allow for air circulation under and around the container.

If your normal routine changes for any reason, for example, you stop riding for a month or you move your horse from pasture to barn or vice-versa, your horse's diet will have to be modified accordingly. Changes in feed should never be made abruptly, however. A horse needs time to adjust when switching from one diet to another. Consult with your veterinarian, then follow his directions carefully.

Water—As we have discussed, your horse or pony needs fresh water available at all times. If you use a tub or bucket, make sure it is cleaned and filled several times a day, especially in hot weather. Rubber or strong plastic are good materials to use around horses as there are no sharp edges. If you prefer to use a galvanized tub, check it carefully for snags, and line the rim with an old rubber hose. Buckets and tubs should be secured to the stall, paddock or pasture fence to prevent them from being turned over. Bucket holders can be purchased at a tack supply store, but strong elastic cords work just as well. Cords should be snug enough to prevent the horse from getting tangled in them, and secure them to the wall or post with eye bolts, not open-end hooks. Eye bolts can be purchased at any hardware or tack supply store.

For horses and ponies at pasture, two or more watering devices are best. Some horses are shy and afraid to approach the "crowd" around the main tank. An alternative water supply allows timid horses a quiet place to drink.

Another option is to install an automatic watering device whereby the horse can fill the bowl himself whenever he's thirsty. He does this by pushing on a lever, allowing fresh water to flow into the bowl; the float keeps it from overflowing. Horses learn very quickly how to operate an automatic watering device.

If you live in an area that gets cold enough to freeze, be sure to break the ice off the horse's drinking water each morning. Many horses will not do this for themselves, thereby failing to get the water their bodies need.

5

CARE OF THE HORSE

Whether you buy a horse of your own or ride a lesson horse at a riding school, you'll want to know how to give the horse the proper care.

Looking after a horse is a big responsibility, but your job will seem easier if you develop a regular routine for daily care. The benefits of a regular routine are threefold.

- *First,* realize that horses respond very well when they know what to expect from you. By developing and following a daily routine, your horse will get to know you and trust you, and become easier to handle.

- *Second,* you will get to know him. If any irregularities arise, *e.g.,* the horse develops a sore leg, goes off his feed, or seems out-of-sorts, you'll notice it right away and be prepared to take the appropriate action.

- *Third,* it's difficult for you to cover all the bases of horse care if you don't know your tools or don't know how to use them. By establishing a routine, you will get so comfortable with your duties that they will become automatic. You won't spend half an hour wandering around wondering what to do next. Knowing your business saves time, energy, and even money. Let's take a closer look at grooming and the tools you'll need.

Grooming Tools

The main purpose of grooming is to keep the horse clean, but it also tones muscle, stimulates circulation, and contributes to the horse's overall health and fitness. Grooming, then, is an essential part of horse care, and anyone who cannot fit grooming time into his or her schedule would do well to delay buying a horse until they have such time available. In the meanwhile, keep on with your lessons and observe the work done by the grooms at your riding school. You can learn a great deal by watching and asking questions.

If you have decided to buy a horse, you will need grooming tools, and that calls for a trip to the tack shop. It's easy to be overwhelmed by the variety of items available, but you can do a highly effective job with just a few essentials.

- *Halter/Lead Rope*—A secure, well-fitting halter is your most important piece of equipment. Halters and lead ropes come in leather, cotton, and nylon. Lead ropes should have a secure snap and be at least eight feet long.

- *Hoof Pick*—This is used to remove mud, stones, and any other debris from the horse's feet. Always work from the heel toward the toe, and take care not to gouge the center of the foot. This area, known as the *frog*, aids circulation through the foot and leg. To pick up a leg, stand close to the horse, facing the tail. Lean your weight on the horse's shoulder (or hip) as you run your hand along the back of his leg, working downward along the tendons toward the hoof. When he raises his foot, support it with one hand while the other wields the hoofpick. Put the horse's foot down gently when you are finished cleaning, and make sure your own feet are out of the way!

- *Dandy Brush*—A stiff brush used primarily for the removal of mud. A dandy brush works well on pastured horses or ponies who have thick coats, but is too coarse for regular use on sleek, thin-skinned horses. If your horse is kept indoors rather than at pasture, you may need it only to brush mud off the hooves. Hold the brush firmly and use short, vigorous, outward strokes, as if whisking lint off a jacket. This brush to too coarse to be used on the face, around the ears, or inside the hind legs.

- *Body Brush*—Softer than the dandy brush, the body brush is the backbone of all grooming aids. You will use this brush every day to remove dirt and dust from all parts of the body. Put some elbow grease into your work and you'll be surprised at how quickly your horse's coat will shine.

  Short strokes work better than long passes, and brush in the direction of the hair. Because you use the body brush every day, it is advisable to replace it about every six months. The other tools need not be replaced as often.

- *Face Brush*—A small, very soft brush especially for use around the face and ears. On sensitive horses with very fine coats, it works well as an overall body brush. Because this brush is used around the face, replace when it shows signs of wear. Worn bristles can break off and get into horse's eyes and ears. Throw it out and get a new one. A brush is far less expensive than a vet bill.

- *Curry Comb*—A plastic or rubber curry comb, used in a vigorous, circular motion, helps remove loose hair.

Take care to use it only on well-muscled parts of the body such as the shoulders, forearms, and hind quarters. Do not use it on the face, along the spine, or on the legs below the knees and hocks. Use the curry comb directly on the horse *only during shedding season*. Otherwise, use it daily to clean body and face brushes. Clean bristles by drawing each brush across the face of the curry comb. Do this several times during each grooming session. Metal curry combs are also available, but they are too severe to use on a horse or pony. Use them only for cleaning brushes. A rubber or plastic curry is a better choice for a novice.

- *Sponges*—You will need at least two. A small, soft one to clean the muzzle and around the nostrils, and a larger one for giving your horse a bath. If you have never given a horse a bath, ask an experienced horseman or groom to help you. Some horses are afraid of water and can be difficult to handle. Bathe a horse only where you can secure him in cross ties and where a butt-bar can be attached to prevent him from pulling back. Never turn a cold hose on a horse's body. Apply water first on the legs, then the hind quarters, then the chest, neck, and finally the body cavity. Wash and rinse the face with the sponge—do not squirt a horse or pony in the face with a hose. Not only is it frightening to him, a blast of water can damage vision and hearing organs.

- *Sweat Scraper*—After bathing and rinsing, use an aluminum or rubber scraper to remove excess water from the coat. Starting at the neck, behind the ears, pull the scraper along the coat, working toward the shoulder. Always work in the direction of the hair. Scrape the body cavity, belly, and hind quarters. Avoid the spine and withers, and do not use it on the legs below the knees and hocks. Dry the face gently with a soft towel. Groom the tail during bathing by first wetting the hair, then applying conditioner. Separate the hairs carefully with your fingers. Rinse and let dry. Brush gently to avoid breakage.

Photo: Betty Skipper for USPC

Grooming is an essential part of all-around horsemanship. Note utility buckets on the left, water bucket on the right.

- *Stable Rubber*—This refers to any type of cloth or towel used to give the coat a final polish. Always work in the direction of the hair. You can buy these items under various brand and manufacturers' labels, but an old terry cloth towel from home works just as well. Launder on a regular basis and replace as necessary.

- *Utility Bucket*—Use the utility bucket to store your grooming tools. Plastic or lightweight rubber is safer to use around horses than galvanized steel, and doesn't make as much noise when items are dropped in. Some tack shops sell wooden or plastic boxes to hold grooming tools, but a bucket is usually cheaper, easier to carry, and serves double duty if you should need to haul water. When it's time for a bath, mix your shampoo and water in the utility bucket, and use your large sponge to wash your horse. After you are finished, rinse bucket thoroughly before putting it away. You will find many practical uses for a good utility bucket. Note—Do not use your utility bucket as a feed bucket. Get separate buckets for horse's feed and drinking water and do not use them for anything else.

Other grooming items you may want to have handy are: a leather punch; a scissors for opening feed bags (keep them away from your horse); a flashlight; a mitt or towel for applying fly repellent or liniment; an aluminum mane comb for grooming the mane, forelock, and tail (be careful not to pull hairs out of the tail).

Veterinary and Stable Supplies

While you're in the tack shop buying your grooming tools, take that opportunity to pick up the basic veterinary and stable supplies every horse owner should have on hand. As with grooming tools, don't be overwhelmed by the variety of items available. The following basics will get you off to a good start.

- *Fly Repellent*—Many good brands are available, but even the best won't help your horse if you don't apply it on a regular basis. Fly repellent can be sprayed on or rubbed on using a mitt or towel. Most spray-on types need to be diluted with water. You can buy a plastic container with a pump-type spray attachment, mix your fly repellent right in the container, then spray it on. Be careful not to get it in your horse's eyes or nose. Spray the mixture onto a mitt or towel, then gently wipe his face and ears.

- *Hoof Dressing*—If your horse tends toward dry, brittle hooves, you'll want a dressing which puts moisture back into the hoof. If your horse tends toward moist, mushy hooves, you'll want a dressing that acts as a drying agent. As a rule of thumb, if your horse lives and works on dry, sandy soil, use a lanolin-based moisture dressing. If your horse lives and works in damp, soggy soil, use a pine tar-based dressing. If you're not sure of the condition of your horse's hooves, don't buy anything until you've talked with your blacksmith and/or veterinarian. Follow their suggestions.

- *Thrush Dressing*—Thrush is a fungus which can develop in a wet or dirty hoof. If left untreated, thrush can cause lameness. You will recognize its presence by the foul odor emitting from your horse's hoof. Thrush can be prevented by cleaning the hooves daily and by keeping footing and bedding clean and dry. If thrush develops in spite of your efforts, it can be treated in most cases by applying a thrush dressing. Several good ones are on the market, or ask your veterinarian for his recommendation. Read the label and follow the directions for application.

- *Topical Infection/Abrasion Dressing*—If your horse should get a minor scratch, an abrasion dressing can be safely applied. The primary benefit of a topical dressing is that it helps keep flies and dirt out of the wound. For anything other than a minor laceration, call your veterinarian.

- *Shampoo/Conditioner*—Do not use human hair products on horses. Equine shampoo is pH balanced for a horse's skin. Human shampoo is very hard to rinse out of a horse's skin, and can even make him sick. There are many excellent equine shampoo and coat conditioners on the market. Let your budget be your guide.

- *Liniment*—After a workout your horse will welcome a relaxing rubdown. To make a body wash, add 1/2 cup liniment to 1 gallon water. (Use your utility bucket.) Dip your large sponge into the mixture, wring, and apply to neck, body, and legs. If weather is cool or windy, cover horse with a wool cooler and walk until dry. Do not put a horse away when his coat is still very damp. Do not apply liniment if a leg feels unusually warm; liniment will just make it hotter. Ice the leg instead, or run cool water over it for at least 20 minutes. If you don't notice improvement within 24 hours, call your veterinarian.

- *Equine Thermometer*—You can and should learn to take a horse's temperature, but do not try it until you have been shown how by an experienced horseman or your veterinarian. NEVER use a human thermometer; they are not the same. Equine thermometers can be purchased at your tack shop. Knowing how to take a horse's temperature is a valuable lesson to learn. It can help you determine the severity of a horse's illness, and when you report your findings to your veterinarian, he will use that information to guide you as to what you should do until he arrives.

Other all-purpose supplies you can purchase either at a tack shop or drug store are: hydrogen peroxide (good for washing superficial wounds); cotton balls; rubbing alcohol (has the opposite effect of liniment—use full strength or diluted as a wash to cool the legs); petroleum jelly (apply to coat where hair has rubbed off).

Health Maintenance

You can help keep your horse healthy by establishing and following a three-step, semiannual veterinary maintenance program.

- *First,* have your veterinarian treat your horse for worms at least twice a year. He will do this by *tubing* the horse with an anti-worm medication. Tubing is not something you can or should do on your own, but ask your veterinarian if you can use a paste or powder wormer in between professional treatments. Follow directions carefully, and use only the products your veterinarian recommends.

- *Second,* have your horse's teeth checked. Horses often develop sharp points on their back teeth, making it hard for them to chew their food. These sharp points must be filed down. Filing, also known as *floating* the teeth, is essential for good health. As we discussed earlier, if a horse cannot work saliva into his food before swallowing, he cannot digest properly; and this interruption in the digestive cycle can lead to colic. The chances of colic can be lessened by regular worming and floating the teeth. Only your veterinarian is qualified to float the teeth. This is not something you can or should do yourself.

- *Third,* establish a semiannual schedule for your horse to receive his vaccinations and/or inoculations. These are usually given by injection. Again, only your veterinarian is qualified to administer this treatment.

Sometimes a horse needs to be rested completely or worked only lightly after getting his "shots." Ask what follow-up care your horse will need regarding riding, feeding, and turnout.

Do not neglect any part of this three-step veterinary treatment program. It is essential to your horse's health. Remember the old adage: An ounce of prevention is worth a pound of cure. No doubt your horse would agree.

Shoeing and Hoof Care

One of the most important elements of good horse management is regular hoof care. Your horse simply cannot perform his best if his feet hurt. Badly shod, poorly trimmed, or injured hooves left untreated are among the most common causes of lameness.

Every time you groom your horse, examine each foot, top and bottom. Use your hoofpick to clean debris from the sole, being careful not to gouge the frog. Use your dandy brush to remove dried mud from around the top of the hoof, called the *coronet*, and from the bulbs of the heels. Apply hoof dressing as directed by your blacksmith or veterinarian.

The feet should be checked and cleaned before and after each ride, especially after a trail ride. It's always possible to pick up a stone or woodchip along the trail. Check to see that the shoes are not loose or twisted, or that your horse hasn't lost a shoe along the way. If you discover that a shoe is loose, twisted or missing, call your blacksmith right away; and do not ride your horse again until the damage has been repaired. Riding with a damaged or missing shoe could cause serious injury, even lameness.

Your horse should be trimmed and re-shod about every four to six weeks. The horse's age, the type of work he does, and the ground conditions or *footing* on which you usually ride will affect your shoeing schedule. It does not hurt your horse to be shod.

Photo: Hagerty Photo

**It takes many years and hard work to become
a skilled horseshoer**

The shoes are held on by nails, and the nails are driven into the *wall*, the outer-most portion of the hoof.

There are no nerve endings in the wall. Your blacksmith can trim the wall and nail on the shoes without causing your horse or pony any pain. In fact, shoes actually help protect the hooves and are regularly used on riding horses. Some barns do allow broodmares to go barefoot, but if your horse is being ridden or worked, shoes will help protect his hooves.

How Shoes Are Selected

Shoes come in different weights, sizes, and even shapes. Some are flat on the bottom, some are rounded. The height, weight, age, and type of work a horse does, along with the overall shape and development of his legs and hooves, determines what type of shoe he should wear. Race horses, for example, wear very thin shoes made of lightweight aluminum. This type of shoe is called a racing plate. Draft horses, by contrast, wear heavy iron shoes, often outfitted with toe clips and heel caulks to help hold them on. To improve traction for horses working on wet grass, *studs* can be screwed into the shoes. Studs function much like cleats on a golfer's shoes. Studs come in various lengths and sizes, and can be removed from the shoe entirely when not needed.

Many decisions must be made before the actual work of shoeing begins. First, the blacksmith will watch the horse move and ask what type of work the horse normally does. That information will help him decide how he will trim and shape the hooves. When the hooves have been shortened, the blacksmith will select and fit a shoe. The best work is always done by *hot shoeing.* That means the shoe is placed in a forge and heated, then molded to the hoof. The shoe may pass between the anvil and the forge several times before the blacksmith has it just the way he wants it to fit. It takes time, but hot shoeing ensures the most accurate fit. Another type of shoeing is called *cold shoeing* in which a ready-made shoe is simply fitted to the foot. Cold shoeing will do in a pinch, but is not as accurate as hot shoeing for obvious reasons.

A blacksmith must attend shoeing school to learn his or her craft. It takes a long time and is a real art, and anyone who has ever won a blue ribbon knows that part of the credit must go to the horseshoer. Your blacksmith, like your veterinarian, is an important part of your team. Follow his or her advice about trimming, shoeing and hoof care.

6

TACK AND HORSE CLOTHING

When man first began to domesticate the horse, he soon found that he needed some means of controlling the animal's movement. Throughout the centuries, many devices (some effective, some absurd) were developed to accomplish that objective. These various and sundry devices for controlling (and eventually riding) the horse have come to be known collectively as tack.

In contemporary terms, tack generally refers to the saddle and bridle (headstall and reins) and their immediate auxiliaries such as girths, pads, leathers and irons, martingales, and bits. In a separate category, leg wraps, blankets, day sheets, boots and the like are referred to as horse clothing. Items in this latter group being more associated with the welfare and upkeep of the horse.

Bridles and Bits
The earliest bridles were little more than ropes woven of hair, twigs and leaves. These ropes were wrapped

around the horse's lower jaw or around the nose and jaw. Over time, as mankind learned how to tan, cut and stitch leather hides, he developed the browband, crownpiece, throatlatch, caveson, and reins. On early bridles, these pieces were sewn together, but mankind eventually learned how to make metal buckles and these were used to join the various pieces, thereby making the bridle adjustable. That application is still in use today. The various components of a headstall can be shortened or lengthened, allowing the bridle to fit more than one horse.

The history and development of bits is a well-researched topic and most tack shops and libraries carry books on this subject. The following describes five bits commonly used on riding horses.

Snaffle

The snaffle is perhaps the simplest bit for the rider to operate in that it is activated by a single rein. The primary division within the ranks of the snaffle is between those which are joined in the middle (jointed snaffle) and those which are straight (mullen mouth snaffle), the latter being the milder of the two.

Snaffles are made in a variety of weights, ranging from the thin bridoon (used with a double bridle) to the thick hollow-mouth used for schooling young horses. Snaffle mouthpieces come in an enormous variety of styles: roller mouth, slow twist, corkscrew, Dr. Bristol, and twisted wire; and are made from a variety of materials: stainless steel, copper, soft rubber, and vulcanite (a hard rubber).

Snaffle cheekpieces come in a variety of styles including: full cheek, "D" ring, egg butt, and loose ring. (One other snaffle sometimes used on jumpers and horses in the cross-country phase of eventing is the gag, but this is a very sophisticated bit and should be used by advanced riders only.)

Pelham

The pelham combines the effects of snaffle and curb into one mouthpiece. It may seem a little more awkward for the novice rider in that it uses two reins, the wider attached to the snaffle (or upper) ring on the cheekpiece, the thinner attached to the curb (or lower) ring. The end result is that with a pelham, the rider has two reins in each hand whereas with the snaffle, the rider has but one rein in each hand. When the snaffle rein predominates, the affect is much like that of a snaffle bridle—pressure is applied to the corners of the horse's mouth. When the curb rein predominates, it causes the shanks (cheekpieces) to swivel, putting pressure on the poll (the top of the horses head) and brings the curb chain into play under the horse's lower jaw.

Double Bridle

A double bridle is composed of two separate bits: a bridoon and a curb. Both bits fit into the horse's mouth. At first glance, the curb looks similar to a pelham, but on the curb, there is no ring to which you could attach the snaffle rein. The double bridle is used for well-trained dressage horses showing third level or above. It is a rather advanced piece of equipment and a novice rider would do better with a plain snaffle bit or a pelham.

Kimberwick

The Kimberwick gives the leverage effect of a pelham but, like the snaffle, requires only one rein. It has a curb chain as does the pelham, but the shanks are very short and the leverage is considerably less than that produced by the pelham or curb. The mouthpiece comes in various styles and materials, including jointed mouth, mullen mouth, and roller mouth.

Photo: Hagerty Photo

A clean and tidy tack room is a sign of good stable management. Note the bosal-type hackamore on the far right of the bridle rack.

Hackamore

The bitless bridle is perhaps the oldest of all devices. The Spanish hackamore, called the *bosal*, is often made of rope or horsehair, and has a single rein coming from the back of the noseband. The mechanical hackamore is usually made of nylon or leather. The reins are attached to metal shanks, one rein on each side. Contrary to what many people think, a hackamore is not the gentlest or kindest form of bridle. A hackamore operates by putting pressure on the delicate nose cartilage. If used roughly, it can cause a great deal of harm. Unless your horse or pony has been professionally trained to a hackamore, you'll probably be better off with a snaffle bridle. Especially in the early stages of your riding.

Saddles

The saddle is a much more recent invention than the bridle, and stirrups are the most recent invention of all. Elaborate versions of the bridle can be traced to the fifth century, B.C., but it wasn't until the fourth century, A.D. that a saddle was built on a leather-covered wooden frame. Another one hundred years later the first stirrup was attached. Originally, there was only one stirrup, not because men rode side-saddle, but because they saw its usefulness only for mounting and dismounting. They quickly discovered, however, that a stirrup helped the rider balance, and if one stirrup was good, two would be even better. The cavalry liked them because stirrups made it more difficult for an enemy to dislodge a warrior from his horse. The new invention took root, and since the fifth century A.D., all cross saddles have been designed to accommodate two stirrups, one on each side. As with bridles and bits, saddles have a long and colorful history.

Photo: Miller's

Dressage saddle has a deep seat and long, straight flaps

- *Dressage*—the dressage has the deepest seat of all modern saddles. That means the seat is considerably lower than the pommel (front) and the cantle (rear). The stirrup leathers are inset a little further toward the cantle than they are on other saddles, positioning the rider's legs well back under the hips. A dressage saddle often has very long billets, allowing the girth to buckle by the rider's foot rather than up under the thigh. This overall design gives the rider a very secure feeling and allows excellent communication with the horse.

- *Close Contact*—the shallower seat and forward cut of the flaps allows the rider to be in balance with the horse when moving at high speed and over fences. When a horse is jumping, its balance shifts considerably further forward than that of the dressage horse in action, hence the rider needs a saddle which allows him to shift his weight forward in time with his horse. The deep seat and straight flap of the dressage saddle

Photo: Miller's.

Close Contact saddle has a shallow seat and forward-cut flaps

would not allow the rider to move forward enough to be in balance with the movements of a jumper. Likewise, the shallow seat of the forward seat saddle would not position a rider properly for the collected movements of dressage. The close contact is also known as the forward seat or jumping saddle.

- *All-Purpose*—this saddle usually comes with adjustable bars, allowing the rider to move the stirrup leather forward or backward depending on the type of riding he will be doing. The seat is a cross between the deep pocket of a dressage saddle and the shallow seat of a jumping saddle. The flaps are not as straight as those on a dressage saddle, nor as forward as those on a jumping saddle. The girth, however, usually buckles under the rider's thigh as it does on a jumping saddle.

Miscellaneous

All-Purpose saddle combines the deep seat of the dressage saddle with the forward-cut flaps of the close contact saddle

It's a rare horse that goes all the way through its training wearing only a bridle and saddle. Horsemen everywhere are quick to employ artificial aids to enhance their control and improve their horse's performance. Some of the most commonly used aids are spurs, martingales, breastplates, and nosebands.

- *Spurs*—devices, usually of metal, which attach to the heels of a rider's boots. Spurs come in a variety of styles, but the most common is the Prince of Wales. Novice riders should avoid wearing spurs until they have learned to keep their feet and legs quiet and under control.

- *Martingales*—the martingale comes in two styles: standing and running. The standing martingale attaches to the girth and extends forward between the horse's front legs, attaching again at the back of the caveson. Between the legs and the caveson, the martingale passes through a thin strap which goes around the horse's neck. This strap holds the martingale close to the underside of the neck, thereby preventing a foreleg from getting tangled in the martingale. It acts to prevent the horse from raising his head so high that he evades the bit. When green horses are first learning to jump, they often lean on the martingale to help them find their balance. Eventually they learn to carry their own balance and no longer require the aid of a standing martingale. Hunters are often shown in a standing martingale.

The running martingale attaches to the girth as described above and also passes forward through the front legs, but it then forks forming two short straps, each with a ring on the end. The snaffle reins pass through these rings, allowing the martingale to "run" the length of the rein. (Rubber rein stops should be used close to the bit to prevent the martingale rings from catching on the bit.) The effect is to prevent the horse from raising

Photo: Miller's

Horse wearing snaffle bridle fitted with a flash noseband.

his head, but with a running martingale, the action is on the mouth, not the nose. Jumpers may compete wearing a running martingale.

- *Breastplates*—a device for keeping the saddle in place. To visualize the breastplate, think of the letter "V" with a tail and a short strap connecting the two uppermost points of the V. The horse sticks his head through the V, the short strap lays across his neck just above the withers. The short neck strap is attached to "D" rings on either side of the saddle. The tail of the V is a strap which passes backward through his front legs and attaches to the girth. Horses competing in jumping and eventing sometimes use a breastplate which wraps around the front of the horse's chest, thereby giving its purchase on the saddle a lower center of gravity.

- *Nosebands*—the noseband comes in a wide variety of configurations, but its primary purpose, regardless of style, is to prevent the horse from opening its mouth far enough to evade the bit. Jumpers often use a figure eight-style noseband while dressage riders prefer the flash or dropped noseband.

Horse Clothing

Basically, horse clothes are those items which enhance the horse's welfare and upkeep such as blankets, bandages, and boots.

- Blankets—the heaviest ones are water proof and lined with wool. These can be used on horses kept at pasture or with free access to the outdoors. For horses kept indoors, woven or nylon blankets are popular, but non water-proof materials are not suitable for horses kept outdoors.

- Sheets—a light-weight version of the blanket, the day sheet provides warmth in cool weather. The fly sheet (lighter weight than the day sheet) prevents insects from biting and can be worn in warm weather to help keep the horse clean.

- Coolers—a loose-fitting wool wrap which keeps hot and/or damp horses from getting a chill. When horses have been bathed, a cooler should be put on while they dry, especially if a breeze is blowing.

- *Bandages*—if ever there was a catch-all word, this is it. A bandage is not limited to a dressing applied over a wound, as the name would suggest. Rather, it means any wrap used on the legs or tail. A tail bandage keeps a horse from rubbing the hair off its tail, and can be especially helpful when a horse is being shipped in a van or trailer. Leg bandages can be used for medicinal purposes, but are just as frequently used to warm, cool, or support a leg. Ask your veterinarian or an experienced groom to show you how to properly apply a bandage. Never use the type of elastic bandage intended for human use on a horse; they contract too much for equine circulation.

- *Boots*—the primary purpose is to protect the horse's legs from injury. Boots are different than bandages in that boots are fitted items while bandages are simply long strips of material skillfully wrapped around the horse's legs. Boots have shape and form, and each is designed to protect a different part of the horse's body. Shipping boots, for example, reach from the hoof to the knee or hock. They are worn whenever the horse is transported in a van or trailer. Bell boots fit over the front hooves and protect the tender heel area from being kicked by the toe of a hind foot. The horse wears these when being ridden or exercised.

Cleaning and Storing

Care of tack and equipment is an essential part of good stable management. Riding with worn or broken tack is dangerous, and ill-fitting horse clothing can result in sores and injuries. The best approach is to examine all tack before and after each ride. If you notice that stitching is coming loose or that buckles are no longer closing securely, take the item to a saddler and have it repaired before the problem gets any worse. Not only will you save money (extensive repairs get expensive), you'll reduce the chances of having the piece break while you are riding. You can prolong the shine on bits by rinsing and drying them with a soft cloth after every ride.

For proper maintenance of horse tack, you'll need the following items:

- Sponge and utility bucket
- Saddle soap or other leather cleaning agent
- Leather oil and small paint brush
- Mild dishwashing liquid
- Small, stiff brush to remove sweat and hair
- Two clean terry cloth rags (old washcloths are ideal)

Start by disassembling your tack. Remove pad, stirrup leathers, irons, and girth from the saddle. Disassemble the bridle: headstall, reins, and bit. Remove the spurs from your boots.

Draw warm water into your bucket and add a capful of mild dishwashing liquid. Allow bit, irons, and spurs to soak a moment, then rub with a clean terry cloth rag. Rinse thoroughly, especially the bit, and, with your second rag, dry immediately. (Terry cloth absorbs moisture and the nap helps the metal shine.) If you wish, you may apply metal polish to your spurs and irons, but if you buy stainless steel, it shines with just a good rubbing. Never put metal polish on the mouthpiece of your bit. Your horse can pick up chemicals from the polish. When you have finished, lay these items aside.

Next, use the small brush to remove any hair, sweat, or grit from the leather, paying careful attention to the underside of the girth. If you use a breastplate or martingale, it should be brushed and cleaned as well.

Empty your bucket and draw a little fresh water. You won't need much as your objective is only to dampen and rinse your sponge. Wipe the leather with a damp (not soggy) sponge. For general cleaning, apply saddle soap (or a good leather cleaner) to your sponge and wipe again. Don't let the leather get too wet—what you need here is elbow grease, not water. Rub thoroughly and leave all leather pieces in a clean, sheltered place to dry. Do not put your tack out in the sun or next to a heater—the leather will crack. To reduce drying time and protect the leather, ring your sponge well and avoid letting the leather get too wet. When you have finished, let your tack dry for a few hours, overnight if possible. Finally, rub gently with a dry cloth and reassemble.

Make sure all buckles are fastened securely and that the bit is not put on the headstall backward (it's easy to do). Before you ride, check that the bit hangs evenly in the horse's mouth and that your irons hang evenly on your saddle. Readjust cheekpieces and stirrup leathers, if necessary.

Two or three times a year, apply a good leather oil. Use the stiff brush to remove dirt and hair, then wipe all leather parts with a damp sponge. Warm the oil in a double boiler, then brush it on with the paint brush. Rub it in with your fingers. Let dry at least overnight, two nights is better. Wipe again with lightly damp sponge, then apply saddle soap as above. Polish with a dry cloth, and reassemble.

Blankets, sheets, coolers, saddle pads, and bandages need to be kept clean and free from rips. Wash horse clothing regularly in a mild laundry detergent, and make sure all items are thoroughly dry before storing. Unlike leather, cotton items love the sun and can be safely laid out for airing and drying. Keep all items in good repair.

Tack and horse clothing should be stored in a clean, dry environment with good ventilation. Do not expose tack to excessive heat or moisture, and wash all horse clothing items before packing them away in a trunk or tack box. If you take good care of your equipment, it will serve you well for many, many years.

7

RIDING ATTIRE

Perhaps the two most important considerations when selecting riding attire are safety and comfort. By no means is it necessary to wear the latest fashion or the most expensive brand of apparel, but it is worthwhile to invest in a few items. Let's take a closer look at what you'll need to get started.

Protective Wear

For English riding, a well-fitting hard hat with a chin strap is essential. Your skull is fragile and a hard hat will help protect you in the event of a fall or accident. No matter how well you ride or how long you've been around horses, always wear your hard hat and fasten the chin strap.

Photo: Miller's.

A safety helmet, known as a "hard hat," is an essential piece of riding attire

Photos: Miller's

Hunt boots extend to the
back of the knees.

Paddock boots stop just above
the ankles.

Next on the list of essentials is proper footwear. This has nothing to do with fashion; riding boots are designed to give your feet, ankles, and legs the support they need for effective communication with the horse and maximum performance. If you're just getting started, you need not go to the expense of custom made boots, but realize that boots influence performance, so get the best fit you possibly can. Most tack shops offer a good selection and you can choose from rubber boots (excellent for wet-weather riding), hunt boots, paddock boots, or heeled riding sneakers. Never ride in flat-soled shoes of any type; your foot could easily slip through the iron.

Gloves are optional, but they do help protect your hands, and many riders feel that gloves improve their grip on the reins. As with boots, most tack shops have a wide selection to choose from including leather, suede, cotton, knit, and stretch fabrics. For horse shows you'll want leather gloves, but for casual riding, wear whatever feels most comfortable. Hint— Riding gloves fit snug in order to provide the right "feel" on the reins. For your comfort and safety, remove any finger rings before putting on your gloves.

| Leather palms with cotton backs are comfortable in warm weather | All-leather gloves are popular with horse show riders |

If you ride after dark, wear a reflector vest—they make you more visible to oncoming traffic. These vests are lightweight, fit over your clothing, and do not hinder your riding in any way. Reflector leg wraps are also available for your horse's legs, and these, along with a rider's vest, increase your margin of safety.

For Casual Riding

Whether you are going on a trail ride or working in the ring, you'll want to be comfortable. Riding breeches, whether casual or formal, are cut differently than regular pants; specifically, breeches have no inseam. Their unique cut allows them to lie flat under your thighs and legs, thereby avoiding the irritation of sitting on a seam. Many riders find breeches more comfortable than any other type of trouser. Several clothing manufacturers offer a line of riding breeches that look and feel like soft blue jeans. As these pants are machine washable and very durable, you may find them to your liking.

Tee-shirts or sports shirts are always popular, and sleeve length is up to you. If the weather is hot, sleeveless tops are perfectly acceptable for casual riding, but you may want to apply a sun screen on your arms and shoulders to avoid getting burned. Many riders use a sun protection product no matter what the weather.

If the day is cool or windy, you may want to wear a sweater or jacket. However, if you decide to take it off, do *not* leave it hanging on a fence post or on a jump in the ring—the wind could blow it, causing a horse to bolt! Put sweaters, jackets and other personal items away in a safe place.

It's a good idea to leave fine jewelry at home. You don't want to get a beautiful piece of jewelry full of dust and dirt, and if you should loose it on the trail it may be very difficult to locate. If you normally wear a nice watch, you may want to buy an inexpensive sports watch to wear around the barn. As for safety, avoid wearing necklaces or long earrings that could catch on bridle reins or other pieces of equipment.

Some riders like to wear chaps for schooling and trail riding. Many companies offer a good line of ready-made chaps, and these are generally less expensive than the beautiful custom made ones worn by Western show riders. Although chaps *do* improve your grip on the saddle, English riders do not wear chaps in competition. Therefore, if you're planning to show, riding without them on occasion will give you a chance to check your balance and position.

There are several styles of rain coats and outerwear on the market today, and no doubt your choice will be influenced as much by the weather in your area as by personal taste. Riding rain coats, like breeches, are cut differently than regular rain garments. They are cut with a "saddle fan" which protects your saddle and keeps the coat from sliding up your legs. Most tack shops offer a good variety.

For Horse Shows

Attire for competition riding could take an entire book by itself. Let's concentrate on what you'll need for your first schooling show.

Under the rules of the American Horse Shows Association, junior riders may not compete without a hard hat with a chin strap in place. Adult riders also are required to wear a hard hat, although the chin strap is optional.

As for your clothing, teenagers and adults will need breeches and knee-high hunt boots for competition riding. Children may wear jodhpur pants and jodhpur boots. Jodhpur pants should be worn with garter straps and pant clips. Jodhpur boots, like paddock boots, cover the ankle but do not extend up to the knee. Jodhpur boots may be brown or black, but hunt boots most often are black. There are two types of hunt boots: dress boots and field boots. Dress boots are smooth; field boots lace over the instep. Most riders choose dress boots as these can be worn in all phases of English riding. Field boots are never worn in Dressage competitions, but many combined training riders prefer the adjustment capability of field boots for the cross-country phase of eventing.

For dressage shows, you'll need white breeches. In advanced dressage, your jacket must be black, but at the beginner level, your jacket may be navy or charcoal gray. A white ratcatcher shirt is required for both males and females. Men and boys wear either a white stock tie or a regular tie of any dark color; women and girls wear either a white stock tie or a white choker. Your hair should not touch the back of your collar—pin your hair up and wear a net, if necessary. At the beginner level, gloves are optional. If worn, they should be leather and of a dark color. White gloves, top hats and tails are worn only for advanced dressage.

For hunter/jumper schooling shows, you'll need breeches and boots as described above; a ratcatcher shirt, which may be pastel or patterned; a dark jacket (also called a hunt coat); and, for females, a stock pin. The pin is worn on the choker in the center of the throat. Male riders wear a regular tie with a tie clasp. Earrings, if worn, must be small and discreet. Necklaces, if worn, should be kept tucked inside your shirt. Bracelets should not be worn. Gloves are optional.

There is much that can be said about proper horse show turnout, but this will get you started in the right direction. Just be aware that as you advance, turnout will become more critical to your success.

8

FIRST AID
AND SAFETY

Although riding is not considered a contact sport, anyone involved in sports knows that an injury can happen to anyone at any time. Fortunately, most riding-related injuries are not serious, but never take a chance with an injured person. The following guidelines will help everyone deal successfully with an injury around the barn or on the trail:

- *Remain Calm.* The injured rider's recovery may depend on the decisions you make, and it's hard to make accurate decisions when you're flustered. Moreover, your behavior may determine the reactions of others around you, including riders, parents, and spectators, and no one will benefit if people are running around, screaming.

- *Stay In Control.* Resist the urge to move an injured rider to a more comfortable location (such as under a shade tree or into the barn). Moving an injured rider could compound the injury. Unless the person is in imminent danger where they are, let them stay there until help arrives.

Whenever there is any doubt as to the nature or extent of an injury, call for emergency assistance (fire, police, etc.).

- *Catch the Horse.* As soon as possible, catch the rider's horse and get it in off the street—for its own safety as well as for the safety of others. If you cannot leave the injured rider, dispatch someone else to catch the horse and lead it, not ride it, back to the barn. The horse is probably too upset at this point to respond well to an inexperienced rider. Let's not have another accident.

The First Aid Kit

It's a good idea to keep a basic first aid kit on hand at all times. Many pharmacies and sporting goods stores carry well-stocked first aid kits that would be fine for barn use. If you want to put one together yourself, the following items should be included:

- Adhesive bandages of various sizes
- Ammonia caps (for dizziness)
- Antiseptic soap (for washing a wounded area)
- Antiseptic solution (for bug bites, minor scrapes)
- Aspirin
- Blanket to cover injured rider (warmth reduces chance of shock)
- Cold packs
- Elastic bandages (various sizes)
- Eyewash solution
- Gauze pads (various sizes)
- Hank's solution (trade name Save-a-Tooth)
- Sterile cotton sheets (can be cut to fit)

- Scissors
- Tissues and pre-moistened toweletts
- Tweezers (for splinters)
- Utility knife, *e.g.*, Swiss Army knife to take on trail rides

The phone number of the nearest ambulance service should be taped to the inside of your first aid kit. All riders and barn workers should know where the first aid kit is stored, and where it will be kept at horse shows and other events. The best first aid kit in the world does you no good if you can't find it when you need it. Make sure someone knows the location of the closest telephone and always keep a quarter or two in the kit so you won't have to hunt for change in an emergency.

Handling A Dislodged Tooth

Most times when a tooth has been knocked out it can be replanted and retained for life, especially if the tooth has been properly handled. One critical factor determining a successful replant is the care and handling of a dislodged tooth.

The best way to store a tooth is to immerse it in a pH balanced buffered cell-preserving solution such as Hank's or Viaspan® (used for transplant organ storage). Hank's solution (under the trade name Save-a-Tooth) may be purchased over-the-counter at many drug stores. It will store the tooth in a safe container for 24 hours and has a shelf life of two years. With the use of a proper storage and transport container, there is an excellent chance of having a dislodged tooth successfully replanted.

Vision and Corrective Lenses

Your vision, just like the strength in your arms and legs, is an important part of your overall performance, and the demands on your visual system during sporting activities are rigorous. To ride your best, you must know what's behind you, beside you, and in front of you at all times, and this takes a variety of vision skills. If your natural vision inhibits your athletic performance, ask your doctor about corrective lenses.

Today's eye care practitioners utilize a wide variety of lens materials. One such development is the new impact-resistant lens now available for use in prescription glasses. These lenses are cosmetically excellent, reasonable in cost, light weight, and will not shatter if broken.

Another option is contact lenses. Available in hard and soft lens materials, contacts offer many excellent advantages to the athlete. For best results, tell your doctor about the type (or types) of riding that you do. That information will be helpful to the doctor in selecting the best lenses for you. If you wear contact lenses, take your cleaning and wetting solutions with you to all equestrian events, and notify your riding instructor that you are wearing contacts. Instructors, as well as riders and parents, should have a basic understanding of how to remove, insert, or recenter a contact lens.

Getting a foreign object in the eye is the most common eye problem associated with riding. Fortunately, these foreign objects are usually in the form of minor irritants such as dust, dirt, or sand. More serious intrusions, such as a blow to the head, may produce bleeding in or under the skin, causing a "black eye." An ice pack will reduce swelling until a doctor can evaluate the injury.

Care of the Eyes

Fortunately, the eye has a number of natural protective mechanisms. It is recessed in a bony socket, the quick-blinking reflexes of the eyelids and eyelashes deflect most foreign particles, and natural tears wash away most minor irritants. If you *do* get something in your eye, follow these simple guidelines:

- Do not rub your eye or use a dirty cloth or finger to remove the obstruction.
- Irritants can often be eliminated by looking down and pulling the upper eyelid outward and down over the lower lid.
- If you see a particle floating on your eye, you may gently remove it with the corner of a clean piece of cloth.
- Apply an eye wash or tap water to flush out the irritating particle. If the object doesn't wash out, keep the eye closed, bandage lightly and seek emergency professional care.

Whatever your recreational activity, your vision plays a vital role in helping you enjoy the sport and perform at peak efficiency. Your eyes deserve the best of care.

Wrist and Hand Injuries

Injuries to the wrists and hands are most often related to falling, although fingers can be "jammed" in a collision with the horse's neck. To reduce the possibility of wrist and hand injuries, follow these simple guidelines:

- Prior to riding or working around horses, remove your jewelry; especially rings and bracelets.

- Avoid riding with your fingers straight out. Keep your finger tips and knuckles curled back toward your palms, and keep your thumbs resting along the sides of your index fingers. Even when you pat your horse along the neck, keep you hands relaxed; never lock your fingers into a stiff or rigid position.

- Avoid putting a "death grip" on your reins. Hold your reins firmly, but gently. That way, if your horse should stumble, he can pull the reins through your fingers and regain his balance without hurting you.

- Gloves are a good way to protect your hands. If you fall, gloves keep your hands from getting scratched; and while you ride, gloves protect your hands from the reins and weather.

Transporting Tips

To be on the safe side, riders who have suffered an upper extremity injury should be evaluated by their doctor. To safely transport a rider with an arm, wrist or hand injury, follow these simple guidelines:

- A finger with mild swelling can be gently taped to an adjacent finger for protection. Use caution and do not "wiggle" the injury.

- An elastic bandage may be gently wrapped around an injured wrist to give the wrist support. Do not overwrap and do not pull the bandage tight.

- If possible, place a pillow in the rider's lap and allow him/her to rest the injured hand on the pillow. Do not bunch the pillow up around the injury—doing so may put added pressure on the injury.

Ice and Heat Treatments

If someone falls or is stepped on by a horse, elevate the injury (if possible) and apply an ice pack. Use ice instead of heat because coldness reduces both swelling and pain. Leave the ice pack on until it becomes uncomfortable. Allow the injured person to rest for 15 minutes, then reapply the ice pack. Repeat this procedure until any swelling abates or, in more serious cases, until professional medical help can arrive.

In most cases, after two or three days or when the swelling has stopped, heat can be applied in the form of warm-water soaks. Fifteen minutes of warm soaking, along with a gradual return to motion, will speed the healing process right along.

Guidelines for Reducing Injuries

Although no amount of planning and preparation can guarantee a rider will never be injured, there are many things a rider can do individually (and a barn can do collectively) to reduce the possibilities of injury.

- Inspect the facility and equipment for hazards. Make sure all stall, paddock, corral, and pasture fences are strong. Doors and gates should swing or slide firmly, but easily; and all doors and gates should fasten securely. Note—More injuries result from faulty equipment than from falling off a horse!

- Never leave wire, boards, logs, garden hoses, or any farm implements such as hoes, rakes, and shovels where horses can trip on them. Horses panic easily, and if they feel caught in something, their natural inclination is to pull back, vigorously!

- If your barn has jumps or trail course obstacles, check them routinely to be sure they are free from snags and loose nails. Hammer any loose nails back into place and remove any debris.

- Check the rings and pastures on a regular basis. Remove rocks and and fill any holes or low places. When rings and riding trails are well maintained, a horse is far less likely to fall or have an accident. Don't wait for someone else to do it—check for yourself. If something is beyond your capacity to repair, report the hazard to the barn manager or another responsible adult.

- Personal clothing, such as jackets, coats and sweaters, should be put in your car or tack trunk when you're not wearing them. From a horse's viewpoint, a jacket on a fence post becomes a fire-breathing dragon, and may well elicit his most explosive behavior.

- Wear a hard hat with a chin strap whenever you ride.

- Always wear sturdy shoes or boots. Sandals and other casual footwear have no place around livestock. No matter how warm the weather, there are two good reasons to keep your feet covered: (1) going barefoot is a health hazard, and (2) the weight of a horse on your unprotected foot can cause a broken toe or an even more serious foot injury. You realize, don't you, that it's *your* foot that will break, not the horse's!

- For grooming and saddling, horses should be secured in cross ties or properly tied at a hitch rail. Never tie a horse to his stall door or to the barn itself—a horse has enough strength to tear off the door and/or pull down a wall. Don't laugh, it's been known to happen. You or someone else could be badly injured in this type of accident.

- Horses should be walked with a halter and lead rope. A rope looped around a horse's neck does not give you the control you need for safety.

- Remember to warm up and stretch before you ride. If the weather is breezy or cold, keep your body covered and avoid drafts. A proper warm up routine will reduce the possibility of a pulled muscle or other injury.

- Make sure your barn has a first aid kit, and always have a source of fresh water available—both for riders and for horses.

- Keep your voice low and avoid running, especially in barn aisles. Horses have keen hearing and they are easily startled—speaking softly and moving quietly greatly reduces the possibility of an accident.

- If you will be riding out on the trail, let someone know where you're going and approximately what time you'll be back at the barn. Never ride in any area where you are unsure of the footing.

- Always seek prompt medical attention for an injured rider. If you don't know what to do, call for emergency assistance immediately. Do not move an injured rider unless he/she is in immediate danger at that location. If you will have to wait long for assistance, cover the injured person with a lightweight blanket, even a saddle blanket will do. Warmth reduces the chance of an injured person going into shock.

EXERCISE AND PHYSICAL FITNESS

In any sport, your level of physical fitness greatly affects your level of performance. It is no different with riding—top riders are top athletes, and they work as diligently at their fitness training as they do at their riding. It is a grave mistake to assume that the horse does *all* the work and the rider just "sits" in the saddle, essentially doing nothing. Granted, the really great riders are so smooth that they give the appearance of "doing nothing," but every muscle is working constantly, communicating signals and commands to the horse. Your ability to ride smoothly and effectively is directly related to your level of physical fitness; and if you are flabby, winded, overweight, or otherwise out of shape, you will not be able to affect that beautiful "invisible" ride.

It's never too soon, or too late, to begin exercising; and whether your riding goal is to participate in top flight competitions or quiet, relaxing trail rides, you will be a safer, more effective rider if you get your body in good working order. Consult with your doctor before beginning any work-out program. If your doctor approves of your participation, the exercises listed here are especially good for riders.

Warming Up

Regardless of your age, it's important that your body be limber and relaxed before you mount your horse. One of the best ways to limber up is to engage in gentle stretching exercises. One word of caution before you begin—do your warm up exercises *before* getting your horse out of his stall or paddock. The sight of you windmilling your arms in front of his face could cause him to bolt!

When doing riding-related exercises, your motions should be fluid. The stretching exercises should be done at a slow to medium pace, preferably in a warm environment. If there is no barn or other enclosed area where you can stretch and you must warm up out of doors, put a jogging suit on over your riding clothes, and leave it on until you are ready to ride. Remember, also, to drink plenty of fluids, especially in warm weather. Your body's lymph nodes need fluid to carry away impurities. Without fluid, your circulatory system cannot function at its best.

- Start with both feet on the ground, your weight balanced over the balls of your feet. Let your arms hang loosely at your sides. Wiggle your fingers, then gently shake your wrists. Now shake your arms. Rest. Tilt your chin down toward your chest and gently roll your head from side to side, eventually making a complete circle. Rest.

- Raise your arms and "reach for the sky." Roll up on your toes and stretch, reaching as high as you can with one hand. Hold this position for 10 seconds, then reach with the other hand and hold. Repeat this exercise five times.

- Rest your hands on your hips and, keeping your back straight and your head forward, stretch to your left. Hold. Now arch your right arm over your head so that your fingers point to your left and down. Hold. (You should feel a gentle stretch along your right side.) Do the same exercise with your left arm, fingers pointing to your right and down. Hold. Repeat this exercise five times.

- Rest your hands on your hips and bend forward from the waist. Do not bounce. Stretch gently, and hold. Now, tilt your chin down toward your chest. Take your hands off your hips and let your arms hang loosely. Wiggle your fingers and shake your arms. (You should feel a gentle stretch along the backs of your legs, up through your back and neck.) Return to a standing position and rest.

- Do 10 windmills with each arm, one arm at at a time, forward then backward. Now work both arms together, forward then backward. Rest.

Now it's time to stretch your legs. Move to an area where you can freely swing your legs and where you will have something sturdy to hang onto. A bar or fence post will do nicely, but watch for splinters. If necessary, wear gloves to protect your hands.

- Stand with your feet about eight to nine inches apart. Your upper torso should be balanced over your hips, your head up (but not tilted back), and your eyes forward. Your body should be straight, but not stiff. If you are right handed, shift your weight to your left leg and begin the exercise with your right leg. If you are left handed, reverse the order. (You will find your rhythm easier if you utilize your natural balance first.) Hold onto the bar or post with your left hand, and gently swing your right leg forward and backward 15 times. Turn around. Do the exercise 15 times swinging the opposite leg. Rest.

- Hold on to your post and balance your weight over your left leg. Stick your right leg out in front of you, toes up toward the sky, heel no more than six inches off the ground. Now, keeping your back straight but not stiff, push your right heel forward (not down toward the ground, forward). You should feel your calf muscle stretch. Do not bounce. Hold for a count of 10 seconds, return heel and toes to starting position, and lower your right leg to the ground. Balance your weight equally over both feet, and rest. Turn around and repeat the exercise with the opposite leg.

Having completed your stretching exercises, you may wish to finish your warm up with a brisk walk. If the weather is nippy, be sure to keep your muscles warm. The point of stretching is to get the blood flowing and to "loosen" the muscles and tendons. An untimely blast of cold air will negate your carefully executed warm up. Keep your body warm until you are ready to ride.

Walking

Walking is fun, free, relatively painless, and one of the best general purpose exercises there is. Walking is so enjoyable that it doesn't really seem like exercise, yet it improves your cardiovascular fitness, circulation, breathing, leg and back muscles, and posture. Walking can be done either as a follow-up to your stretching routine, or as an exercise in and of itself.

Be sure to wear properly-fitting, shock absorbing footwear. You need to protect your tendons, joints, muscles, and bones from undue concussion, and good walking shoes can help you do that. Your footwear need not be expensive, but it must fit right to be effective. Pay attention to your socks—do they fit correctly, or are they large enough for 'Big Foot?' If your foot slides or if you have excess sock wadded up under your foot, you'll never be comfortable. Improperly fitting socks prevent your foot from correctly distributing your weight in the shoe. This, in turn, limits the shoe's ability to provide the shock absorption and protection it was designed to provide. Moreover, socks and shoes that are too loose or too tight can rub on your foot, causing painful blisters. When you put on your riding boots, blisters prevent you from stepping down in your heels the way you should, resulting in a less effective and less safe ride. Pay as much attention to your exercise footwear as you would to your riding boots—good shoes and socks are not an expense, they are an investment in your health and well-being.

When you walk, keep your back straight and your head and eyes forward. Some people prefer to bend their elbows and hold their hands in front of their bodies, others prefer to let their arms swing from the shoulder. Your step should be vigorous and your stride comfortable.

In the beginning, you may be most comfortable walking on flat ground. After you have increased your stamina, try adding a few gentle hills to your walking routine. Don't turn this into a mountain climbing venture or you'll be building the wrong muscles for riding. Remember, riders want long, elastic, sinewy muscles, not bulk. Concentrate on exercises that encourage an open, flowing range of motion.

Now it's time to get your horse ready and go for a ride.

 **10**

RIDING BASICS

Good horsemanship is an art. No one, no matter how famous, ever learned to ride overnight. Riding well requires many years of practice and experience. Even top riders such as Olympic and World Cup competitors know that no matter how many blue ribbons they've won, every time they get on a horse, they are "learning." These riders know that effective riding requires communication and harmony between horse and rider—and communication is a two-way street. Intelligent riders allow every horse they ride to communicate its feelings to them. This is not an idle exercise. What the rider learns from the horse enables the rider to bring out the horse's best performance.

Even if you are a beginner, it's not too soon to learn this valuable lesson. Whenever you approach your horse, pay attention not only to his physical condition but his mental state, as well. Does he seem a little nervous today? Perhaps you should turn him out for 15 to 20 minutes before you ride. Does he seem a little sluggish? Perhaps a trail ride would help. Does he shy at some particular spot in the ring? Maybe something is catching his eye that usually isn't there. Investigate these things and act on them accordingly.

Letting your horse communicate with you is not the same as letting him get away with "bad" behavior. The former enables you to be an active, effective horseman; the latter makes you a passenger on an unhappy ship. You maintain the upper hand by having more than one way to solve a problem. For example, let's say your horse is acting a little sluggish. You know your horse is in good health, but today he's moving like a sleep walker. One way to solve that problem in an effective, productive way is to go out for a trail ride. It's amazing what a trail ride can do to perk up a sluggish horse. In no time at all, your horse will feel revitalized and move forward with energy and impulsion. Return to the stable and continue your ride as planned. You maintained the upper hand by identifying the problem and employing an effective, productive solution. Top riders know that looking, listening, and responding appropriately always works to the rider's advantage.

Tacking Up

After you've given your horse a good grooming, you're ready to put on the saddle, bridle, and any additional equipment. This procedure is known as *tacking up*. If your horse wears boots or bandages, put those on first. If you use a martingale or breastplate, put it around the horse's neck, then reattach the cross ties to the halter.

The saddle is put on from the left side. Lift it over the horse's back, and gently place it just above the withers. Now, slide it back toward the tail until it lies slightly behind the withers. You will feel the saddle "nestle" into place. If you go back too far, lift the saddle and repeat the procedure. Never pull it forward as this would cause the hair to lie in the wrong direction. Make sure the saddle pad is not bunched or twisted. The pad should fit up into the gullet of the saddle; it should not be pulled tight across the horse's spine. If the pad isn't right, start over. Don't fret if you have to do this a few times, you will soon get the hang of it. Never mount up if the pad and/or saddle are not properly adjusted. Ill-fitting tack can give a horse a sore back.

Photo: Betty Skipper for USPC

A young rider adjusts his saddle and girth before mounting

Once the saddle is correctly seated, reach under the horse's belly and pick up the girth (it will be hanging from the billet straps on the right side of the saddle). Make sure it hangs straight and is not looped over a post or other object. Pull it toward you. (If you are using a martingale or breastplate, run the girth through the loops.) Now, buckle the girth to the billet straps on the left side of the saddle. Leave the irons run up until you are ready to mount.

To put on the bridle, stand on the left side of the horse's head. Unbuckle the halter, slip it off the horse's face, and rebuckle it loosely around the neck. Holding the bridle by the crownpiece, lay the reins over the horse's head. This serves two purposes: 1) it gives you some control should the horse start to walk away, and 2) it prevents the horse from getting his feet and legs tangled in the reins. Next, hold the caveson and crownpiece in your right hand and with your left, slip the bit into the horse's mouth. Secure the crownpiece over the ears, left ear first, then right ear. Pull the horse's forelock out of the browband. If necessary, adjust the cheekpieces so that the bridle fits comfortably. Fasten the throat latch. If you are using a standing martingale, loop it through the caveson before fastening the caveson. Fasten any additional tack such as a dropped noseband or a curb chain (make sure all links lie flat). Unbuckle snaffle reins, loop them through the rings of your running martingale, and rebuckle.

If you must turn away from your horse for any reason, such as to put on your riding boots or lock your tack box, put the halter on *over* the bridle and attach cross ties to the halter. Never attach cross ties directly to the bridle. For safety's sake, both yours and the horse's, ask your instructor to check that everything is properly adjusted.

Mounting and Dismounting

If you're not already wearing your hard hat, put it on and fasten the chin strap. Release the horse from the cross ties, lift the reins over his head, and lead him to the mounting block. If your barn doesn't have a mounting block, lead him into the ring and close the gate. Lead the horse from his left side. Hold the middle (buckle) of the reins in your left hand and place your right hand 8 to 12 inches from the bit. Look toward the direction you are moving, walk smartly, and allow the horse to follow you. Do not look at the horse as this only encourages him to stop. Your assistant should go with you and soon it will time for his or her help.

Photo: Gary R. Coppage for USPC

Pony Club members demonstrate the correct way to lead a pony or horse

When you have reached the mounting area, pull your irons down and put the reins back over the horse's head. Check the girth and tighten, if necessary. Your assistant should stand on the right side of the horse and take hold of the bridle. You should stand on the left side, close to the saddle. Gather the reins in your left hand. Turn slightly toward the tail, and with your right hand, turn the iron toward you. Place your foot in the iron, resting your toe on the girth. Grasp the cantle (back) of the saddle with your right hand, grasp the mane with your left hand (don't drop the reins), and push off with your right foot. Swing your right leg up and over, taking care not to kick or gouge the horse in any way. Sink gently into the saddle, do not flop down like a lead balloon. Adjust your feet in the irons and gather the reins in both hands. When you feel secure, ask your assistant to release the bridle and step away from the horse. You are now ready to ride.

To dismount, have your assistant hold the bridle from the right side of the horse. Place the reins in your left hand and push down on the horse's neck with your right hand. Take your right foot out of the iron and swing it up and over the horse, behind you. Slide your right hand to the cantle (back) of the saddle, balance yourself a moment as you slip your left foot out of its iron, and drop gently to the ground. Push yourself slightly away from the horse as you drop. Continue to hold the reins in your left hand as you dismount or your horse will be loose and could walk away. Should you accidentally drop the reins, your assistant can hold the horse until you regain control.

Before returning to the grooming area, run the irons up the stirrup leathers and lift the reins over the horse's neck. Lead as discussed above.

Stretching and Balancing

Stretching exercises done while mounted are very beneficial to a novice rider. They improve suppleness and balance, and increase a rider's sense of security and self-confidence. Beginner riders of any age should have a knowledgeable assistant hold the horse while the rider performs the exercises. Begin the exercises with the horse standing still.

- Sit in the center of your saddle, grasp the pommel (front) with your hands, and stretch your toes toward the ground. Now stretch your heels toward the ground. Repeat. Without rising from your saddle, stretch your upper body toward the sky as you stretch your legs toward the ground. Visualize yourself as a rubber band, stretching upward from your waist, and downward from below your waist.

- When you feel secure, remove your hands from the pommel and place them on your hips. Repeat the toe and heel stretching as you slowly raise your arms out to your sides. If you start to feel insecure, lower your arms, get organized, and try again. Your goal is to raise your arms over your head while your legs are stretching down, down, down.

- Extend your arms over your head and wiggle your fingers. Now, pretend you are climbing a ladder, stretching one arm higher, then the other. In your waist, you will feel your body shift gently from side to side. Your goal is to keep your seat level in the saddle as your upper body stretches from side to side. This exercise improves suppleness, and suppleness is what enables a rider to follow the motion of the horse.

- Place your hands on the pommel again. Keep your legs straight and push your heels down. Now, move your left leg forward, toward the horse's shoulder. Hold onto the pommel so you don't tip backward. Return the left leg to its normal position and move the right leg forward. Alternate and repeat. When you feel confident, try moving both legs forward at the same time.

- Hold onto the pommel and swing one leg forward toward the horse's shoulder as the other swings back toward the tail. Be careful not to kick the horse. Your legs should slide smoothly along the horse's sides. For this exercise you may find it helpful to place one hand on the cantle (back) of your saddle and keep one hand on the pommel. Alternate hands. Your goal is to keep your back straight and your seat bones in contact with your saddle.

- Place your hands on your hips and face straight ahead. With your back straight, bend forward at the waist. How far can you go? Don't let your legs swing back behind you. Your goal is to be flexible in your upper body while keeping your lower body quiet and stationary. Return to an upright position. Get organized, now lean backward. If you feel insecure, hold onto the pommel and try again. Repeat. Take your time; this is a stretching exercise, speed is not the objective.

- Repeat the above exercise, but this time, stretch your arms out in front of you and try to touch your horse's ears. Stretch your arms behind you and try to touch his tail. Return to an upright position. Stretch one arm forward over the horse's mane, the other behind you toward the tail. Alternate and repeat. Your goal is to develop a supple waist, a relaxed back, and a secure seat.

When you feel confident doing these exercises at a standstill, ask your assistant to lead the horse at a walk. Repeat the exercises while the horse is walking, starting with whichever one was easiest for you. If you lose your balance, ask your assistant to stop the horse immediately. If you're not too tired, reorganize and try it again; however, if you're not used to riding, your body may be telling you it's had enough. Do only what feels comfortable, and save the rest for another day.

Photo: Dawn Johnson for USPC

A helpful assistant makes learning easier and more fun

Walking

After you have warmed up with a few stretching exercises, sit in the center of your saddle and place your feet in the irons. Before you walk forward, glance down. You should not see your toes. If you do, your feet are too far out in front of you. Roll forward onto your seat bones and bring your lower leg back underneath you. Do not rest your weight on your derriere. You are riding a horse, not an easy chair. Sit tall and push your heels down.

Gather your reins so that there is a slight loop between the bit and your hands. If you start to fall back in the saddle, the loop will prevent you from catching the horse in the mouth. Don't worry right now about your hands, their time will come. As a beginner, your primary objective is to develop a secure seat.

Gently squeeze your legs against the horse's sides. Do not kick, squeeze, and keep your heels down. If necessary, you may give a little "cluck." As the horse walks forward, relax and allow your body to follow along. If you brace against the motion, you are telling the horse to stop.

Walk along the perimeter of the riding arena. When you have made one complete circuit, ask the horse to stop. Brace your back, close your legs gently along the horse's sides (so that he steps forward into the bit), and close your fingers on the reins. If necessary, say "whoa" in a soft voice. Do not pull on the reins. If the horse fails to stop, don't get excited, simply try it again. Spend several days going from halt to walk to halt before moving on to the trot. Your horse needs time to understand you, and you need time to develop your seat.

Trotting

Because the trot has a more vigorous up-and-down motion, it is easier to learn to ride this gait when the horse is controlled by another person. Your riding instructor or assistant will stand in the middle of the ring and control the horse via the *lunge line*. One end of the lunge line is attached to the horse's bridle, the other is held by the groundperson. The horse moves comfortably in a controlled 30-foot circle. The rider does not have to "steer" and is free to concentrate on learning to ride.

Place your reins in your weak hand and grasp the pommel firmly with your strong hand. Squeeze your legs a bit more vigorously than before, and add a cluck, if necessary. As the horse starts to trot, pull yourself up and slightly forward, then gently return to your normal seated position. At a trot, a horse moves his legs in diagonal pairs. As one pair reaches forward, the other pair is planted on the ground. The sequence reverses with the next step, the legs that were on the ground now reach forward.

At the trot, the rider rises from the saddle on one sequence, and sits on the next. This sequence of rising and falling is known as *posting*. A rider posts either on the left diagonal or the right diagonal. You are posting on the left diagonal when you rise as the left foreleg reaches forward. You are posting on the right diagonal when you rise as the right foreleg reaches forward. Don't worry about right and left diagonals just now. Concentrate on finding and maintaining a rhythm. Rise, sit; rise, sit; rise, sit. Hold your upper body erect and lean forward from the waist. If you need help, grasp the pommel and pull yourself out of the saddle. Count one-two, one-two. Keep your heels down and your shoulders back. Don't get discouraged, it takes time to master the trot.

Cantering

Many riders, even beginners, believe the canter is the smoothest of all gaits. Because the canter is a three-beat gait, the horse's lifting motion is smooth and gradual, thereby producing that wonderful "rocking chair" effect for which the canter is famous. It's best to begin on the lunge line. Concentrate on your riding and let the groundperson control the horse.

The stretching exercises you did to loosen your body will prove most beneficial. At the canter, a rider's seat bones remain in contact with the saddle, and the horse's motion is absorbed through the rider's lower back. To achieve this, the head and shoulders must remain stationary. If they tip forward, your balance will be compromised and you'll find yourself gripping with your calves. This is wrong. Your legs should lie gently along the girth, and contact should be evenly distributed between your thighs, knees, and lower legs.

Glance down to see that your toes are not visible. If they are, roll up onto your seat bones and get your lower legs back where they belong. Push your heels down. Low heels will help anchor your seat and keep your legs in the proper position.

Do not worry about your hands right now. Work from the lunge line until you perfect your balance, rhythm, and timing. Concentrate on keeping your legs underneath you, your heels down, and your seat bones in the saddle. Let your lower back become loose and supple, and keep your shoulders straight. Do your stretching and balancing exercises at least twice a week, and practice posting the trot for at least five minutes every time you ride.

Photo: Gary R. Coppage for USPC

**Hard work pays off with a happy, obedient horse
and a textbook-perfect ride**

When you have finished riding, dismount, run up your irons so they don't catch on anything, lift the reins over your horse's head, and walk him back to the cross ties. Put the lead rope around the horse's neck and remove the bridle. Slip the halter on, fasten, and secure the cross ties to the halter, one on either side.

Unbuckle the girth, disengage martingale or breastplate straps, and remove the saddle. Slip martingale or breastplate over the horse's head and reattach the cross tie.

Finally, remove any boots or bandages. If the horse is warm, walk him until he's cool. Return to the cross ties. Clean and paint the hooves. Groom thoroughly, then put away. Feed and refill water tubs. Wash and dry bit. Put away all tack and horse clothing.

 **11**

GLOSSARY

Like all sports, riding has a lexicon of its own. Being familiar with the language of riding will help you understand the sport and make you a better horseman or horsewoman. Using official terms to phrase a question or explain a situation will facilitate your communication with instructors, veterinarians, blacksmiths, tack and feed dealers, and horse show officials.

Aid—a signal used by a rider to give instructions and directions to his horse. Aids are further divided into two catagories: *artificial* and *natural*.

AHSA—American Horse Shows Assoc. The governing body of equestrian events in the United States. Other equestrian organizations can be AHSA Affiliate Members and establish their own rules, so long as those rules do not conflict with those of the AHSA.

Anvil—a heavy iron block with a smooth face, usually of steel, on which horseshoes are shaped.

Artificial Aid—any piece of equipment, such as crop, spurs, or martingale, which the rider employs to help convey instructions to his horse.

Automatic Timer—an electrical apparatus used for show jumping and other timed events. The horse breaks an electronic ray as it goes through the start, triggering the mechanism which starts the clock. As the horse goes through the finish, it breaks another ray which stops the clock.

Barrel—that part of the horse's body between the forearms and the loins.

Bay—a dark-skinned horse with a black mane and tail, and normally black markings on the legs. Bays range in color from a yellowish-brown coat (golden bay), to a deep mahogany red (blood-bay), to a dark blackish-brown (seal bay or seal brown).

Bit—a device, usually made of metal or rubber, attached to the headstall and reins, and placed in the horse's mouth. The bit helps the rider regulate the position of the horse's head and is one aid used to control pace and direction.

Black—a dark-skinned horse with a black coat, mane and tail. No other color may be present. White markings on the legs and/or face are common.

Blacksmith—Also known as a horseshoer or farrier. Blacksmith is an old term which originally applied to any artisan whose medium was iron. Now used to denote a trained professional who trims and shoes horses.

Body Brush—used to remove dust from a horse's coat.

Bran—a by-product from milling grain, wheat and oat bran being the most common used for horse feed. Served dry, bran helps to control diarrhea (see *Bran Mash*).

Bran Mash—made by pouring boiling water over a bucket of bran and allowing it to steep. Add salt and a tablespoon of brewer's yeast. Stir and serve warm. When served damp, it acts as a laxative and aids digestion. A good evening meal for tired or stressed horses (see *Bran*).

Breastplate—a device, usually of leather, which fits around the chest and attaches to the saddle and the girth. Used to prevent the saddle from slipping backwards.

Bridle—that part of a horse's tack which includes the headstall, bit, and reins.

Browband—that part of the headstall which lies across the horse's forehead, below the ears. Prevents the bridle from slipping backwards.

Brush Box—a fence used in hunter and equitation classes. Can also be used in jumper classes, but is then usually enhanced by posts and rails, making for a more difficult fence.

Canter—a three-beat gait, faster than a trot, but slower than a gallop.

Cavalletti—small jumps used in the basic training of a horse to encourage it to lengthen its stride, improve its balance and strengthen its muscles. Also used to teach novice riders how to jump.

Caveson—that part of the headstall which goes around the horse's nose. Also called a noseband.

Cheekpiece—1) that part of the bridle to which the bit is attached at one end and the crownpiece at the other, every bridle has two cheekpieces, one on either side; 2) side pieces of a bit to which the reins are attached.

Chestnut—a horse with a gold to dark reddish-brown coat, usually with matching mane and tail. Some chestnuts have a flaxen-colored mane and tail. On no account can the mane and/or tail be black. That would make the horse a bay, not a chestnut.

Clear Round—a show jumping or cross-country round which is completed without incurring any jumping faults or time faults.

Colic—an abdominal distress, often caused by an obstruction in the digestive tract. Can be very serious. Consult veterinarian immediately. Follow his/her directions regarding care and treatment.

Collection—shortening the pace by using a light rein contact and gentle pressure from the legs. Collection helps the horse find its balance by teaching it to bring the hind legs well forward, thereby supporting its body.

Colt—a male horse less than four years old.

Combination—an obstacle consisting of two or more separate elements, but which is numbered and judged as one obstacle. Combinations usually have only one or two strides between elements.

Combined Training—a comprehensive test of horse and rider covering three phases: dressage, cross-country, and stadium jumping; held over a period of one, two or three days, depending on level of difficulty.

Contact—the link between the rider's hands and the horse's mouth made through the reins.

Crownpiece—that part of the headstall which fits over the top of the horse's head, behind the ears.

Curb Bit—when the rider applies pressure to the reins, the shanks of the curb bit swivel, thereby tightening the curb chain and exerting pressure on the poll. The horse drops his head to release the pressure.

Curb Chain—a lightweight chain of flat rings, fitted to each side of a pelham or curb bit. Increases leverage and control.

Curry Comb—made of rubber or metal. Used primarily to clean bristles on body brush. Metal combs should not be used on a horse. Rubber combs may be used in a circular motion on shoulders, neck and hind quarters.

Dam—the female parent of any horse or pony (see *Sire*).

Dandy Brush—stiff-bristled brush used to remove mud.

Double Bridle—a bridle consisting of two separate bits, a snaffle and a curb. Bits may be operated independently for maximum effect.

Dressage—the art of horse and rider working in complete harmony to perform all movements in a balanced, supple and obedient manner.

Equine—1) a horse; 2) of, or pertaining to, a horse.

Eventing—(see *Combined Training*.)

Farrier—a person who trims and shoes horses (see *Blacksmith*).

Fault—a method of scoring errors such as knockdowns, refusals, or time penalties.

FEI—the *Fédération Equestre Internationale* (International Equestrian Federation), is the governing body of international equestrian events, including the Olympics and World Cup. All national federations must comply with the rules of the FEI during international competitions.

Fence—refers to an obstacle to be jumped on a horse show or cross-country course.

Filly—a female horse less than four years old.

Floating—filing sharp points off the back teeth of an adult horse.

Foal—a baby horse of either gender.

Forge—a device for heating horse shoes so that the metal can be shaped to fit the hoof.

Forelock—the long hair on top of the horse's head which hangs in front of the ears (see *Mane*).

Frog—located on the bottom of the foot. Aids circulation to foot and leg and improves traction.

Gelding—a male horse not used for breeding.

Girth—a device passed under the belly and buckled to both sides of the saddle to hold it in place.

Grand Prix—literally, Grand Prize. A sport performed at its most difficult level.

Gray—a dark-skinned horse with a coat of black and white hairs mixed together; the whiter ones becoming more predominant with age.

Green—a horse which has not completed its training.

Groom—n.) any person responsible for looking after a horse; v.) to clean and care for a horse.

Hackamore—a bitless bridle of two types: mechanical or bosal. On mechanical type, reins attach to shanks extending from the caveson; on bosal type, reins attach directly to the back of the caveson.

Halter—a headpiece, to which a rope can be attached, for leading or tying a horse.

Hand—a linear measurement of 4 inches (10cm). Used in measuring the height of a horse from the ground to the withers, the fractions expressed in inches, *e.g.*, a horse measuring 65 inches is 16 hands, 1 inch; written as 16.1 hands.

Headstall—the parts of a bridle which fit around the horse's head and face.

Hoof—refers to the entire foot of a horse.

Hoof Pick—a hooked metal device used for removing stones and debris from a hoof.

Horse Show—a competition to test the qualities and capabilities of horses and riders.

Hunter—a horse which competes over fences or carries a rider in the hunt field. Show hunters are judged on performance, manners, way of going, style of jumping, and (in some classes), conformation. Hunter classes are not judged on time (see *Jumper*).

Irons—(see *Stirrup Iron*.)

Jumper—a horse which competes over fences. Jumpers are judged on their ability to clear the obstacles and (in certain classes) judged on time. They are not judged on how they look or behave (see *Hunter*).

Jump-off—in show jumping, a round held to decide the winner among competitors tied for first place after the previous round. The jump-off course is usually shorter and also judged on time. The horse with the least number of faults and the fastest time wins.

Kimberwick—a bit where a single pair of reins controls the mouthpiece; but unlike a snaffle, a kimberwick has a curb chain.

Lead Rope—a cotton, leather, or nylon rope with a clip at one end for attaching to the halter. Used for leading or tying a horse.

Lunge Line—a cotton or nylon rope, 25-35 feet long. Attaches to the halter and is used to exercise the horse. With the handler standing in one place, the horse moves in a large circle around him/her.

Mane—the hair along the top of a horse's neck, extending from behind the ears to the withers (see *Forelock*).

Mane/Tail Comb—long-toothed comb for cleaning and combing the mane and tail.

Mare—a female horse four years of age or older.

Martingale—a device which attaches to the girth at one end and either the caveson (Standing martingale) or the reins (Running martingale) at the other end. Helps the rider control and balance the horse.

Muck Out—to clean and remove soiled bedding from a horse's stall.

Mustang—a wild horse.

Natural Aids—the rider's body, hands, legs, and voice. Used to give instructions and directions to the horse.

Near Side—the left side of a horse's body. A rider usually mounts and dismounts from the near side.

Noseband—(see *caveson*.)

Off Side—the right side of a horse's body.

Oxer—a fence composed of two elements, with a space in between the elements. The two elements are jumped in one single effort, and scored as one fence.

Pastern—That part of the leg between the fetlock joint and the hoof. Along with tendons and ligaments, pasterns function, in part, as shock absorbers.

Pelham—a bit which combines the effects of the curb and the snaffle. The snaffle rein attaches to the top rings, the curb rein attaches to the bottom rings. The curb chain attaches to the "eye" of each shank.

Pony—an equine not exceeding 58 inches in height (14.2 hands) at the withers.

Post and Rails—a type of obstacle consisting of upright posts between which are laid horizontal rails. In jumper and equitation classes, these rails may be multicolored; in hunter classes, they must be of a solid color.

Prix des Nations—literally, Prize of Nations. An international team show jumping competition. Four riders per team, each jumping the course twice. Show jumping is scored like golf, the lowest score wins. Best (lowest) three scores from each team are then added together, the fourth score from each team is discarded. The team with the lowest combined score wins the event.

Red Flag—a marker used to denote the right-hand extremity of a course or an obstacle. It must always be passed with the red flag to the right of the horse and rider (see *White Flag*).

Red Ribbon—a red ribbon of any material tied into the tail of a horse known to kick; used especially in the hunt field, but should be used on any kicker ridden in the company of other horses.

Refusal—stopping in front of, or passing beside, any obstacle intended to be jumped.

Rein Back—at the rider's command, the horse steps backwards while being ridden or driven.

Reins—long, thin straps or ropes attached to the bit or caveson (see *Hackamore*). Used by the rider to guide and control the horse.

Ring—a riding arena of any size, shape or dimension.

Roan—a horse having a black, bay or chestnut coat with a mixture of white hairs, especially on the body and neck, which modifies the color.

Saddle—a seat for a rider on horseback, made in various styles, sizes and weights, depending on its purpose.

Saddler—a person who makes, repairs, or sells equipment for horses and riders, including saddles, bridles, and boots.

School—n.) an enclosed area where a horse may be trained or worked; v.) the act of training a horse toward a particular goal.

Sire—the male parent of any horse or pony (see *Dam*).

Snaffle—possibly the oldest form of bit. A single bar, jointed, hinged, or straight, with a ring at each end to which the reins are attached. The variations on the snaffle are endless, but all have the same general action which is to apply gentle pressure against the corners of the horse's mouth.

Sole—the bottom of the foot. The frog is located in the middle of the sole, extending from the bulbs of the heels forward, halfway to the toe.

Sound—a horse free from any illness, disease, blemish or physical defect which might impair its usefulness or ability to perform, either under saddle or in breeding. Genetic defects are considered unsoundnesses and a stallion or mare with such defects would be classified as unsound for breeding.

Spread Fence—an obstacle which is wide, *e.g.*, a hogs back or a water jump.

Stable Rubber—a cloth of any material used for polishing a horse's coat; a cloth used for general stable maintenance.

Stallion—a male horse, age four or older, suitable for breeding.

Steward—an official of the horse show's governing body responsible for seeing that a competition is conducted according to the rules. In the U.S., Stewards are licensed by the American Horse Shows Assoc. (see *AHSA*).

Stirrup Iron—a device suspended from a saddle to support the rider's foot.

Stirrup Leather—an adjustable strap by which a stirrup iron is attached to a saddle, one on each side.

Sweat Scraper—a curved metal or plastic blade used to scrape water or sweat from a horse's coat.

Teeth—when fully mouthed, a horse has 40 teeth: 12 incisors (6 in ea. jaw), 4 canines (1 ea. side of upper and lower jaws); and 24 molars (6 above and 6 below on ea. side. Fillys and mares lack canines.

Three-Day Event—(see *Combined Training*.)

Throat Latch—a narrow strap on the headstall which fits loosely under the horse's throat. Prevents the bridle from slipping over the head.

Thrush—an inflammation of the frog characterized by rot and a foul smell. Requires cleaning the sole and treating with anti-thrush medicine.

Time Allowed—period of time in which a rider must complete a show jumping course without incurring time faults. A rider incurs time faults at the rate of 1/4 fault for every one second over the time allowed (see *Time Limit*).

Time Limit—the maximum time in which a rider may complete a show jumping course. A rider exceeding the time limit is eliminated (see *Time Allowed*). Note the difference between Time Allowed and Time Limit.

Trot—a two-beat gait in which the horse's legs move in diagonal pairs.

Unsound—a horse which has any defect which makes it unable to perform its intended function (see *Sound*).

USET—United States Equestrian Team. A non-profit organization which prepares American riders and horses for international competitions such as the Olympics and the Pan American Games.

Vertical—an obstacle whereby all its component parts lie on one vertical plane.

Walk—a four-beat gait. The walk should be rhythmic and energetic with the hind legs reaching well under the horse's body.

Wall of the Hoof—that part of the hoof which is visible when the foot is placed flat on the ground. It is divided into the toe, the quarters (sides), and the heel.

White Flag—a marker used to denote the left-hand extremity of a course or an obstacle. It must always be passed on its right-hand side, the white flag is to the left of the horse and rider (see *Red Flag*).

Withers—the highest part of a horse's back; the area at the base of the neck.